Great Castles

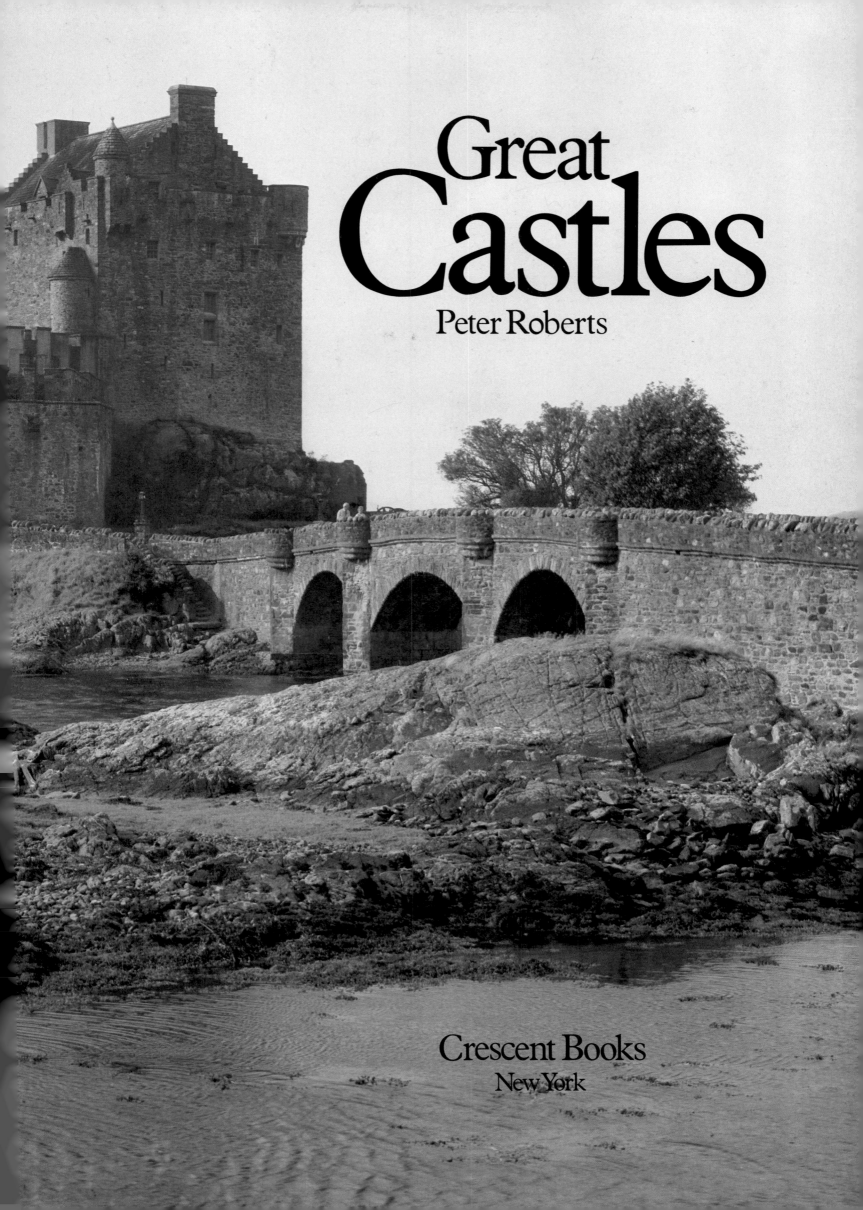

Great
Castles

Peter Roberts

Crescent Books
New York

The author and publishers would like to express their sincere appreciation to the following persons and organizations for their generous help in documentary and historical research, for facilitating the inspection of certain castles, and for advice in the taking of photographs:

Austrian National Tourist Office; Belgian National Tourist Office; Bord Failte; British Tourist Authority; Cyprus Tourist Board; Czechoslovak Travel Office; Danish Tourist Board; Department of the Environment; French Government Tourist Office; German National Tourist Office; The Goethe Institute, London; Italian State Tourist Office; Netherland National Tourist Office; P & O Normandy Ferries Ltd.; Swiss National Tourist Office; Wales Tourist Board; The Welsh Office; Mr. Anthony Davis; Herr Koseck, Burghotel Sababurg; Mr. Fred Kingsley; Herr Walter Kranz, Press Office, Vaduz, Liechtenstein; Mrs. Jane Moffett of Illinois, USA; Mr. Piet Sillevis of Newcastle Emlyn; and especial thanks to Mrs. Karin Mitra for translations, interpreting and helping to raise so many castle portcullises. . .

Photographic acknowledgments
Belgian National Tourist Office, London 66–67, 70–71; Bildarchiv Foto Marburg 72; Biltmore Company, Asheville, North Carolina 121, 122–123, 123; E. Boudot-Lamotte, Paris 112; British Library, London 12 top; British Tourist Authority, London 23 bottom, 24; J. Allan Cash, London 41, 44 top, 76, 77, 88–89, 100; Country Life, London 21, 33, 36 top, 36 bottom, 37; Crown copyright – reproduced with permission of the Controller of Her Majesty's Stationery Office 25, 32 top; Hamlyn Group Picture Library 18–19, 52; Hamlyn Group Picture Library – Country Life Books 35 bottom left; Hammond Castle Museum, Gloucester, Massachusetts 124 top, 124 bottom; A.F. Kersting, London 23 top, 26–27, 35 top, 98–99, 116, 118–119; Mansell Collection, London 109; Pierpont Morgan Library, New York 12 bottom; Scala, Florence 51 bottom; Spectrum Colour Library, London 28, 38 top, 72–73, 108, 110–111, 114–115; Tony Stone Associates, London front cover, back cover, title spread, pages 34 bottom, 126 bottom; U.S. Department of the Interior, Washington D.C. 120–121, 125; Woodfin Camp-Marc & Evelyne Bernheim, Washington D.C. 127; ZEFA, London 126 top, 126–127; ZEFA – R. Everts endpapers, pages 111, 113; ZEFA – M. Fugère 75; ZEFA – A. Liesecke 114; ZEFA – J. Pugh 35 bottom right; ZEFA – K. Scholz 117; ZEFA – Studio Benser 84.

The illustrations on p.17 and p.19 top are reproduced by Gracious Permission of Her Majesty Queen Elizabeth II.

All other photographs are from the Peter Roberts Collection.

Front cover:	Neuschwanstein Castle, Germany
Back cover:	Segovia Alcazar, Spain
Endpapers:	Château de Josselin, Brittany
Title spread:	Eilean Donan Castle, Highland, Scotland

Copyright © The Hamlyn Publishing Group Limited 1981

First English edition published by
The Hamlyn Publishing Group Limited
London · New York · Sydney · Toronto
Astronaut House, Feltham, Middlesex, England

Library of Congress Catalog Card Number: 81-66724

This edition is published by Crescent Books
distributed by Crown Publishers, Inc.
b c d e f g h
Printed in Italy

CONTENTS

Introduction   6

Life in the Castle   11

Castles of the British Isles   17

England   17

Wales   28

Scotland   33

Ireland   38

Châteaux of France   39

South West France   57

Castles of Belgium, Holland and Denmark   66

Belgium   66

Holland   72

Denmark   75

Castles of Central Europe   77

Germany   77

The Rhine   88

Austria   97

Switzerland   100

Liechtenstein   106

Czechoslovakia   108

Castles of the Mediterranean and the Levant   109

Spain   109

Italy   113

Cyprus   116

Syria   116

Castles of America   120

Glossary   128

Introduction

'An Englishman's home is his castle' is an adage with a solid background since man has always been forced to find, or build, some sort of shelter against the weather, predators and enemies.

What, then, is a castle? The answer is complex. In English the word castle is unequivocal. In most dictionaries it is defined as 'a fortress, a fortified dwelling'. A dwelling of some size and substance may be called a manor, a palace, hall, house or mansion, but if it has no fortifications – crenellations, machicolations, archières, gatehouse and other machinery designed to deny entry, it is not, in English, a castle. To call a fort a castle would be equally wrong. A fort is specifically designed to deny entry to unwelcome visitors, but does not fulfil the function of a home for its occupier. A true castle also had to fulfil other obligations. It was the social focus and the judicial centre of the region and was also usually the place where sentence was executed.

In French the nearest we can get to the word castle is château. There is, however, a difference in definition allowing, for instance, the great edifice at Fontainebleau to be included. In English Fountainebleau would be termed a palace, with its lakes, its great inviting staircase-entry, its stucco décor and vast areas of glass. But in French, any notable building of some antiquity, be it on the grand scale of Fontainebleau or of the modest Château d'O, a late Gothic gem in Orne, may be called a château. The term châteaufort, which would be more appropriate for castles such as the heavily fortified Bonaguil or Fougères, is rarely used today for the castles of France.

In Germany a similar duality of meaning exists. A schloss may be a palacial Herrenchiemsee, or a stronghold hanging on to the edge of a mountainside like Schloss Vaduz in Liechtenstein, with its

The château d'O in the Orne, northern France, was built in 1505 by Jean d'O and added to during later periods, losing its defensive character in the process.

6

Left: Chantilly, France, a château but not a castle. The present château was built in 1875–82 on the site of two 16th century châteaux.

Below: Bonaguil near Cahors in France, a true châteaufort.

once-commanding field-of-fire over the Rhine Valley. The use of 'Burg' defines more sharply a primarily defensive structure with a secondary purpose of domestic accommodation (from the Latin *burgus*, a stronghold). These are the castles one may see towering over rivers and hillsides, which were used as 'toll-stations' or regional protectors – castles such as Burg Eltz, and the Rhine castles Burg Gutenfels, Burg Katz, Burg Reinfels, all of them built to house their large and militant families and their maurauding garrisons, as well as to terrorize passing river traffic.

Germany has also to contend with the castles built in the Romantic period of the mid-to-late 19th century. Of Bavaria's clutch of castles, many of them were built by poor half-mad Ludwig II, King of Bavaria, whose passion for building escapist fairytale castles, Neuschwanstein, Herrenchiemsee, Linderhof, ended only with his self-inflicted death. These are rather like most of the castles in the United States which are castles by courtesy only, their prime purpose having been to accommodate their occupiers in a manner to which few of them could have been accustomed, and their battlements, their loopholes, drawbridges, portcullises, constructed merely for the pleasure of owners and guests.

Five hundred years after the last of the Roman legions had left northern Europe, the Normans were busily enlarging their own territory and building castles to consolidate their gains in various countries. In Britain, they constructed their forts in obviously strategic positions, often on the site of old Roman strongholds which occupied natural positions of strength.

Charlemagne had done the same in his Frankish Empire three hundred years before the Normans, but these were more often designed for the mutual protection of the religious orders who lived in them, rather than for military reasons.

The Norman castles were motte-and-bailey design, a system which relied mainly on the age-old defensive qualities of the earthwork, and were very similar to those built by the Franks centuries earlier to keep the Vikings at bay. The motte, a large circular mound of earth – usually about 15 metres (50 feet) high – dug up from the area immediately surrounding it, was the core of the complex. The ditch thus created around the flat-topped hillock would form an additional defence. On the motte some form of strengthened timber shelter or tower would be built, a home and also a last refuge for the occupants of the 'castle' during an attack.

An outer wall of wooden palisades was thrown up round an area surrounding the motte – a larger but lower plateau – called the bailey. In the bailey, behind the protection of the outer wall, the

Above left: Herrenchiemsee, Ludwig of Bavaria's castle-palace based on the design of Versailles.

Above right: The keep at Cardiff Castle, showing the Norman motte-and-bailey layout.

Right: A Norman stronghold tower overlooking the River Teifi in remote West Wales.

more lowly of the castle establishment would build their huts and, if the bailey was large enough, establish a small flock or herd. A bridge of sorts connected the motte and bailey so that those who worked in the more vulnerable bailey could flee to greater safety in the event of attack. Motte-and-bailey construction details may still be seen in many castles of the Norman and later periods – castles such as Windsor, which has two baileys (now known as the Upper and Lower Wards) and Warwick, in which one can clearly see the raised mound that served as the original castle's motte and keep.

A development of the simple motte with its wooden structure was the later Norman 'donjon' or great tower such as the White Tower at the Tower of London. This weighty stone keep was built by William the Conqueror to subdue the population of London, and was a prototype for many more of its kind in Britain. For security reasons, its entrance was on an upper floor of the 30-metre (98-foot) high tower (reached by an outside stairway) and its walls were 4 metres (13 feet) thick at the base.

A century or so later, when the crusading armies of Europe had returned from the Levant where they had learned much of defensive construction, a marked development in castle design became apparent. The keep was often taller and less square. It served as a lookout tower as well as a refuge, and was surrounded, not by a single wall, but by two or three which were supported at the corners by towers from which the outside of

Above: By the 16th century the influence of the Renaissance was beginning to show in château design and décor. Here the Château of Azay-Le-Rideau shows the Renaissance theme superimposed upon the old military style.

Below: Archières were designed to protect the bowman without unduly narrowing his field of fire. Later some were enlarged into loopholes for castle guns.

the walls could be observed and protected. Between the often concentrically-built walls were the lists – narrow alleys in which attacking forces could be trapped, should they scale or breach an outer wall.

Castles, still built to protect from non-explosive weaponry, continued to develop along the lines of the improved Norman castles. Cruciform archières could allow a bowman a wider field of aim and more strategically placed machicolations allowed the dropping of unspeakable things on the heads of an enemy. Such developments continued until the early 15th century, when the entire concept of defence was changed by the introduction and development of firearms, a technological advance that was soon to bring heavy cannon into siege warfare, completely upsetting the balance of power between an army in the field and a force sheltering behind now vulnerable castle walls that could be blasted into rubble within a few days.

The castle defence system had to be swiftly adapted to prevent an enemy from getting too close to its immediate environs. Corbelled machicolations disappeared. Towers became shorter and stronger to accommodate heavy cannon. Moats were widened, wall-walks and tower-roofs were strengthened to carry bombards and mortars, and round holes were cut into arrow-slits to allow a culverin-barrel through.

The role of the castle as an impregnable structure was over. Armies had become more mobile, cross-country routes had become more negotiable, and castles, if they put up a fight at all, could be by-passed. Battles were fought in the open and few commanders would waste time besieging a garrisoned stronghold.

By the 16th century once-formidable castles had often become the country residences of royalty and its court. Older castles, dismantled, or in a state of ruin, were used as sites or foundations for newer châteaux that paid lip-service to the castle proper with mock machicolations and bartizans but which were, in fact, places of leisure. Such châteaux include Azay-le-Rideau and the graceful Chenonceau.

Life in the Castle

In peace or in war, the castle of the Middle Ages was a closed, self-contained world; a miniature city or a small state. Each had its suzerain lord, its hierarchy within keep and bailey, its strict pecking-order of master and servants. Life in the castle was always hard, often perishingly cold, and with its tight-packed complement, frequently short. Quarrels flared in the confined living space, disease swept through staff, garrison and family alike. Hygiene as we know it today was almost absent. There was a medieval latrine system of the garderobe situated over a brattice and sometimes using the plentiful European rainfall to help keep it clean, and the herbal remedies that for centuries had been the mainstay of medical treatment.

The keep usually contained the armoury, the great hall, kitchens (which were sometimes separate buildings), pantry, servants' quarters and a room to which the lord and his lady would retire, although a great bed in the hall used often to suffice. Often a keep or bergfried (central tower seen in some German castle layouts) would have an underground store room designed to keep perishables for a prolonged period, and a well-shaft if a water supply, one of the basic essentials of siege warfare, had been located. This store room was sometimes used to house prisoners – hence the word dungeon, from donjon.

The keep was the inner sanctum, the final secret of the castle, used in normal times for family life, and during a siege as a refuge. Its design

Above: Machicolations – a stone platform built out around a tower or curtain wall with holes in the floor through which missiles could be dropped.

Below: The medieval kitchen can always be indentified by its large fireplace. The food store was often located in the lower room of the donjon or keep.

The great hall of a castle was used for dining, and as a servant's dormitory. Here the King of Portugal entertains John o' Gaunt.

was usually a heavily-guarded secret. Entry could only be negotiated by those closely associated with it and in more than one recorded case, the owner of such a newly-built castle keep rewarded his architect by lopping off his head, just to keep its secret in the family.

For every day of war there were a thousand of peace. Monotonous weeks and months of a simple life largely dictated by the cycle of the seasons. The day could be spent by the overlord and his chevaliers in the forest hunting with hawk or bow. Rarely did the lord know how to read or write, for such learning was considered more fitting for clerks and clerics than for noblemen.

Jousting or exercising skill-

A trebuchet was a giant sling which used counterweights for propulsion. This 13th century print shows one in use during a siege.

Above: A covered wall-walk at the top of a curtain wall.

at-arms was a frequent diversion, and a very necessary one for survival in combat. Jousting in its various forms could cost a knight considerable sums – his armour and his horse were often the prize that went to the victor. Skill with arms was improved by hours of practice, perhaps mounted on a 'school' horse, cantering up to a 'straw gallows' (a rope-hung straw-filled sack) and lunging continually with sword, axe or lance at the swinging target. Pages and squires,

men-at-arms and knights; all knew that such constant exercise would be vital in the event of an attack.

It should also be realized that in the Middle Ages, combat, particularly a full-scale battle, was the cherished pastime of the more bloodthirsty and many leaders of the day would rejoice in the prospect of a pitched battle, being nothing more than a rude game to those in power.

Eating, drinking and quarrelling, were the prime entertainments at

the close of the day in the castle. Wine and beer-making was a major occupation, and a large castle could consume prodigious quantities – the intake at Heidelberg Castle for instance was some 2,000 litres a day during a prolonged period of high life.

As for food, a 12th century list reads: 'The castle should be provided with spelt and wheat, and haunches and bacon, and other meat put in storage, sausages and entrails, meat puddings, pork,

mutton, beef, lamb . . . '

In large well-organized establishments, butlers and stewards would see that vast quantities of food would be regularly served in the great hall. By no means did all the food consist of rough-cooked wild game. In the late Middle Ages, some courses would be served in the form of delicately flavoured pâté or mousse, moulded into the shape of the animal or bird from which it was made. And if a visit from the monarch took place, then the feast that the castle's master was obliged to provide, could bankrupt him.

When under siege, the inhabitants of the castle would become self-sufficient, using its stores of food and ammunition and able to replenish food supplies only from moat and dovecote. Although castles have been called impregnable, in truth there was no such condition. A besieging force need only to wait for starvation to

Top left: If an intruder managed to get beyond the portcullis into the entrance of a castle, a missile from a meutrière – murder hole – in the ceiling of the passageway could effectively dispatch him.

Above right: A basic defence principle – no windows or apertures near ground level. This is one of the near-impregnable walls of Vèves in Belgium.

Left: A drawbridge, or pont-levis, first line of denial to unwelcome visitors and sometimes supported by as many as three portcullises.

force the defenders into submission.
However, few invaders had time or
patience to await events. They had
risks of their own to run which
included low supplies and disease.
Also long sieges were notorious for
encouraging men to wander off back
home. Events had to be moved
along.

Methods of attacking a castle
were several. So were the ways of
preventing successful attack.
Within the confines of the castle,
squareplan keeps and towers had
developed into missile-deflecting
round structures by the end of the
12th century. They were built with
machicolations, a series of holes
beneath a built-out platform over
the walls from which defenders
could drop stones, hot oil and other
discomfiting objects on the heads of
any who were near the base of the
castle walls.

Merlons and embrasures, the
solids and voids of a crenellated
battlement, were useful for firing off
a quick arrow. The merlon could be
quickly dodged behind whilst
reloading. A longbow or crossbow
was usually used although
longbows, ideal for open battle,
were somewhat awkward to handle
in castle defence. Archières, or
arrow-slits, could be designed for a
wide field of fire when sited
correctly. A long slim slit from the
outside, the archière widened out in
a broad 'V' inside, giving the
bowman a sweep of vision. Lateral
cuts in the archière could enlarge
even more the angle of fire.

Walls were built high to defy
escalading – attacking the castle by
means of ladders – and meutrières
(murder holes) were sited in the
ceilings of archways and entrance
alleys to allow defenders to fire
down on intruders. Windows and
vents were few near the ground, and
of course moat, drawbridge and
portcullis were there, the
conventional machinery of denial to
the unwelcome. Hoardings or

Top: A selection of arms and armour at Vaduz Castle in Liechtenstein.

Above: Walls were built high to defy escalading. Crenellated curtain walls helped protect defending archers.

covered ways, protecting the wall-walk above the curtain walls (the defensive walls of the castle, also called the chemise, or in its entirety, the enceinte), were often constructed of wood and placed in position for battle only, allowing ease of movement for wall-top defenders.

The gatehouse of a castle was often built some way out in front of its main entrance as a necessary defensive measure. From this barbican – which could be in the form of a gate and bailey outside the walls and leading to the main entry via an exposed bridge – armed defenders could ensure that any arrival could be vetted before being allowed to enter the castle proper.

Escalading was the first and most favoured method of attacking in force. Long ladders cut from a local copse were placed against the walls in numbers and scaled in force. These were fairly easily dealt with if the defending garrison was strong in numbers. One hearty heave and a ladder and its occupants would crash down. A wooden ram, protected by a penthouse or sow (mobile roof) could be used to beat down a door if accesses were first made possible, perhaps by filling in the moat with rubble, a task also performed under cover of a protective shield. If a door proved too massive, it could be weakened with the ram followed by setting fire to a cart loaded with wood soaked in animal fat and set against the entry.

Mining was also extensively used. The system was simple. A weak point in the walls would be found, preferably with some 'dead ground' (an area out of sight of the castle defenders) at its approaches so that men could work in comparative safety. Sappers would then pick away the lower stone courses, levering out the masonry and making a tunnel into or under the wall itself, supporting it with wooden props as they progressed. Again dry brush would be brought up, placed into the tunnel and ignited, eventually burning down the props and, it was hoped, bringing much of the stonework of the wall down with them. It often worked, with one hazard. Defenders, hearing the digging, would also dig towards the sound of activity, and a ghastly underground combat could ensue.

Great siege engines such as the tall siege-tower or belfry could be used if the attacking force was large enough. Trundled to the wall, its drawbridge was let down and its men charged out on to the allure. Here numbers counted and a battle could be won in a few brief moments of skirmish.

Powerful weapons using projectiles were employed on both sides of the besieged castle wall. The trebuchet and ballista worked respectively on the principles of counterpoise and torsion, slinging huge rocks at the castle walls, or the besiegers camp, with almost the speed and effect of cannonballs. The mangonel (from which the word gun is derived) was another feared torsion-based missile projector.

When, in the 14th century, the first crude firearms appeared, the entire picture changed. Roundelades or *pots de fer* (iron jug-shaped pots) were the first chancy cannon, weapons which fired bolts only very approximately in the direction of the enemy. But accurate heavy guns were developed extremely rapidly and by the middle of the 15th century, artillery had become a potent weapon. The day of the castle as a major defence position was over.

Warfare itself was also becoming more fluid; there were now numerous cross-country routes and if a hostile castle were to be found on an invader's journey, it was simply by-passed. In 1418 England's Henry V took several months to capture by siege the towns of Rouen and Cherbourg. Just a few years later in 1449 the French took considerably less time to accomplish the re-conquest of Normandy using powerful and accurate artillery.

Castles of the British Isles

England

Windsor

Windsor Castle, ancient and venerated, principal residence of England's monarchs since before the days of the Norman conquest, is England's most historic fortress, the largest inhabited castle in the world.

About four years after the Battle of Hastings, William, Conqueror of Britain, had built a motte-and-bailey defence on a bend in the middle reaches of the River Thames, west of London, part of the ring of castles built to defend the approaches to the capital in a time when rivers were often the only way of travelling across a region. William's wood-and-earthworks castle was sited on a chalk outcrop, an escarpment rising to 30 metres (100 feet) above the river and affording good views in most directions.

Henry I rebuilt the first rough defence works and Henry II, his Plantagenet descendant, strengthened them, and added a shell keep on the raised motte, the first of the stoneworks at Windsor. Known as the Round Tower, it was then about half its present height, which owes much to 19th century reconstruction. Although many new buildings – royal apartments, chapels and military quarters were built inside the great walls during the past eight centuries, the two separate baileys (now called wards) are still clearly visible and the original layout is virtually undisturbed.

A strong outer ring of walls had been started in the 12th century under Henry I, curtains supported by heavy flanking towers. The western walls, last to be constructed, were protected by the circular towers on the roadside of Windsor's busy main street today.

Before the walls were finally completed, Windsor Castle suffered one of its two sieges. Richard the Lionheart's brother John had challenged the right of the King to his royal title whilst Richard was held captive abroad. He was besieged at Windsor by loyal barons for a month.

The second siege also involved the notorious John. He had signed the Great Charter of England – the Magna Carta – and slyly arranged to modify parts of it to his own advantage. John managed to placate his attackers on both occasions, and since then Windsor's defences, like many other English castle walls, have never been breached. This, it must be admitted, was largely due to the more fluid type of skirmishing in a country that suffered no foreign invaders after the Normans but was often in rebellious but evanescent conflict with the government.

After Edward III (1312–77), who had a special affection for the castle, had added various royal and domestic apartments for the Court's regular use, shifting and changing the military emphasis of Windsor to that of a royal palace, he arranged to build accommodation in Windsor's lower ward for some twenty-six 'knights of worth in the land', who were to be members of his new order of chivalry, the Order of the Garter. About a century later the Order's lofty Saint George's Chapel was built – although uncompleted until Henry VIII lent a hand in raising what was by then a Gothic edifice in the perpendicular style. Today Saint George's Chapel, perhaps of all Britain's historic monuments, attracts more attention from serious students of history than any other.

Waterloo Chamber in Windsor Castle. An annual banquet is still held here to commemorate the historic victory over Napoleon.

The Civil War which put Oliver Cromwell at the head of Government, saw Windsor's clergy ejected and in their place Roundhead troops stationed in the castle, their horses stabled in the Chapel. Sacred treasures were melted down into bullion to

maintain the military forces. During this time King Charles I was held at Windsor Castle before the grim business of his execution at London's Whitehall. On 9th February, 1649, the decapitated king was buried by his friends and his son in Saint George's Chapel.

After the Restoration, Charles II took a hand in the castle's structure, dismantling parts of the old Upper Ward and building new wings in the then fashionable Baroque style, one which was later considered tasteless. Georges III and IV

renovated the castle, more sensibly restoring it to much of its medieval glory.

Windsor Castle, from which Britain's Royal family takes its name, has been the stage for many a scene of Britain's history. It is still, after nearly a thousand years, the home of the monarch, a living part of the continuing history of the kingdom.

Bodiam

When Edward III finally returned to England from France and his

victories at Crecy, some of his noble followers declined to accompany him back over the Channel. One such knight was young Sir Edward Dalyngrigge, who had been granted a castle in France in return for his services in warfare against Charles of Blois. When Dalyngrigge eventually sailed for his homeland he was rich with success from the spoils of the Hundred Years War, and was appointed to high office by the king (by then Richard II). A personable man, he married Elizabeth Wardedieux, who

Above left: Windsor Castle, sited on a strategic bend of the River Thames west of London, the largest inhabited castle in the world.

Above right: Windsor, the Queen's Audience Chamber. Its ceiling, painted by Verrio, depicts Queen Catherine of Braganza, wife of Charles II.

Right: 'Permission to Crenellate' was given to Bodiam Castle's owner by King Richard II. It thus became in 1386 part of England's defences.

brought as her dowry a manor on the Kent-Sussex borders near the banks of the River Rother.

Dalyngrigge applied for permission to fortify his new home. Richard agreed, for this was an accepted way of defraying some of the costs of defending the realm, a privilege granted, however, only to the most loyal of subjects. Sir Edward built what in effect was a new fortified dwelling, designed to comply with the licence.

Bodiam, sited on a small lake, became in 1386 a complex of quadrangular plan with corner towers, with additional central towers on two walls. The main entrance was originally approached via an exposed causeway and barbican, which necessitated crossing the lake and several draw-bridges. No enemy had a chance in a thousand of survival if

he chose to attack the castle from this direction.

Bodiam was on the Cromwellian slighting (dismantling) list and suffered some damage, but was restored by a more recent owner, Lord Curzon. It is considered to be one of the most enchanting medieval castles in England.

Warwick

Early proof of the importance of Warwick Castle, the formidable stronghold on the bank of the River Avon, occurs in the reign of Henry III. Because of its recognized strength and its strong strategical position on the river, Margary, daughter and heiress of the 3rd Earl, Thomas Newberg, was required to give solemn assurance that she would not contract to marry any person but one in whom the King had complete confidence.

Warwick Castle was an ancient and established stronghold, even in Henry III's time. Originally a settlement, gaining protection from the river, with an earthen rampart as further defence against the Danes and their ilk, Warwick, probably then called Waerinc Wic, 'dwellings by the weir' existed as early as the 6th century. William of Normandy built the first fort there in 1068, a motte-and-bailey complex. Numerous occupants, Earls of Warwick and others, have built and rebuilt it since.

Warwick Castle, extended and modified continually over the centuries, slowly changing from fort to country mansion though retaining its strong defensive appearance, is an amalgam of various styles from Norman to Renaissance. The raised mound of the motte (mistakenly called

Ethelfreda's Mound) is still visible and the courtyard is bounded by the ramparts and ditch of the old Norman bailey.

The Norman Conquerer gave the castle to Henry de Beaumont, granting him the title of Earl of Warwick. Since then Warwicks of various lineage have been part of English history.

Richard Beauchamp (1401–39) Earl of Warwick, tutor to young Henry IV, was also his aide in France during the time of the French victories and responsible for the judicial burning at the stake of Joan of Arc. Another Warwick, Richard Neville, called Kingmaker, played a significant part in history during his 15th century tenure. His two daughters were, at the time of his death, married to the younger brothers of Edward IV. Isabel, who had inherited the castle, had

Above: The armoury at Warwick Castle.

Left: Warwick Castle in the English Midlands. Its original motte-and-bailey layout can still be seen by visitors.

married the Duke of Clarence (later to be put to death at the Tower by drowning in a butt of wine), and Anne had wed Richard, Duke of Gloucester, who was later to be crowned King Richard III.

Earlier, in the ebb and flow of the wars of the Roses, the Kingmaker had actually imprisoned Edward IV at Warwick for a period but a brief two years later the tide of military fortune changed and Edward captured the castle, proclaiming himself monarch again in March 1471.

King Richard III, a capable ruler much maligned in history, visited the castle several times and would, had his reign been more peaceful, probably have made Warwick the royal home.

Leeds

'The most queenly castle in all England' was the description given by an 18th century writer to one of Britain's most ancient and historic fortresses. Leeds Castle, near Maidstone in England's garden county of Kent, reclines with regal grace upon two close-set islands in the centre of a small lake, screened by trees and meadows, and invisible to the passing eye.

Leeds, one of the stateliest fortified dwellings in England and judged by many to be the most beautiful castle in the world, was

built more than eleven centuries ago, before the Conquest, before Windsor Castle, before the great Tower of London, the stronghold of a Kentish Thane since A.D. 857. Rebuilt in stone by Henry I, it was the home of the much-loved Spanish wife of Edward I, Eleanor of Castille, and given to the state during his reign. Leeds Castle saw service as a royal residence for some three hundred years, a 'lady's castle', occupied by no fewer than eight medieval queens of England.

Edward II, later attacked and took it when its owner Lord

Above: Leeds Castle in England's 'Garden County', Kent. Home of eight of England's medieval queens, it is considered to be one of the most beautiful castles in the world.

Right: Few fortified sites in England are as impressive as Dover, its multiple defenses low-profiled against the sky.

Badlesmere refused to offer his hospitality to Edward's Queen Isabella ('the She-wolf') of France and Edward beheaded him there. In 1382 Richard II, his grandson, gave Leeds to Anne of Bohemia, his eight-year-old bride.

Leeds Castle was home to Queen Catherine de Valois, just twenty-one years old in her widowhood. Here she met and fell in love with her Clerk of the Wardrobe, a young squire called Owen Tudor. They secretly married and together founded the Tudor dynasty; their child Edmund was to be the father of the Tudor King Henry VII. His son, Henry VIII, brought his Anne Boleyn here in happier days. More than three centuries later Queen Victoria's eldest son (later Edward VII) stayed at Leeds, and the castle played a part in modern history during the last war when Field-Marshall Montgomery worked and planned here for the great D-Day offensive.

It later passed, through Royal Grant and Purchase, into the hands of some famous English families of the 16th and 17th centuries – the Saint Legers, the Culpeppers, the Fairfaxes. More recently, Leeds was bequeathed by its half-American owner Olive, Lady Baillie, to the country, after she had restored much of its fabric to its late medieval state. Now, Leeds, dower castle of so many queens, 'that beautiful palace in Kent' as King Richard II called it, has been brought back into the mainstream of life and history as a medical conference centre. In honour of its first royal owner, Leeds castle still flies the flag of Eleanor of Castile, alternating with that of its last owner, Lady Baillie.

The square keep at Dover Castle, one of the finest in Europe, was built by Henry II in about 1185.

Dover

Often the first glimpse of Britain for the seaborne visitor is the castle of Dover, its bulk hugging the top of the white chalk cliffs that face the chill waters of the English Channel.

Traces of defensive earthworks from the Iron Age have been found on this site. A Roman lighthouse was certainly here, and a Saxon church is still here. The fort at Dover was strengthened by the Normans, developed during medieval times and modified for contemporary warfare during the threat of invasion from Napoleon's France. Dover Castle had been an active military position until twenty years ago, and a bulwark against Britain's enemies for a thousand.

England's King Harold had promised William, Duke of Normandy, to build a castle on Dover's eastern cliffs. He had also reluctantly promised England's crown to William upon the death of his father, Earl Godwin of the West Saxons. Harold did not keep his promise and William conquered England. Dover Castle, near the site of the Battle of Hastings, resisted fiercely, but unsuccessfully, and its castellan was beheaded. Dover was given into Norman hands as a prize.

Henry II, the Plantagenet king, rebuilt this castle in a time of rapidly advancing warfare techniques at a cost of £7,000, an enormous sum then and the greatest ever spent on a castle of the time. Some of his work is still seen today – the keep and the inner ward. Henry also built the small chapel in the castle keep, in penance for his murder of Archbishop Thomas Becket. His design for Dover Castle is the first example of concentric defences in either Britain or Europe.

Richard I stayed at the castle on his way to the Crusades, and he, too, later spent a considerable sum on the castle. This fort was used by Charles I in 1642, but the lawful sovereign lost it when Cromwell's forces took it by trickery.

The castle, since then unused as a royal residence, was handed over again to the military in about 1690 and re-garrisoned. Its unique historic chapel of Saint Mary was used by the quartermaster as a coal store.

Later, in 1804–5 Napoleon's forces were assembled in Boulogne, just across the water from Dover Castle, poised to invade. By then the castle's towers had been lowered and reinforced as gun emplacements, increasing the fire-power of the castle considerably. The invasion never came.

More recently, in 1940–45, Dover Castle was again under fire from guns across the channel. Dover suffered much from heavy shelling by German forces stationed on the French coast but the castle was never seriously damaged. Some say that it was spared on Hitler's orders; that he wanted to use the castle as his English home.

Left: The massive Constable's Gate at Dover Castle in Kent was built in 1221 by England's Henry III.

Right: St. John's Chapel, the Norman church in the White Tower, heart of the Tower of London complex.

Tower of London

Still garrisoned after almost a thousand years of existence, the Tower of London, the heart of which is the White Tower built by William the Conqueror, is at the life-core of British history. Its story is the story of the nation, albeit in some of its more grim and bloody aspects. Here the kings and queens of England lived when the Tower was used as a palace. And here some of the kings and queens of England were lodged during their last cheerless days before their deaths by the axe. Here indeed many heads, noble and common, fell on the block (a macabre item that may still be seen by visitors) after condemnation for treason or heresy.

Through the sinister river entrance known as Traitor's Gate have passed many an historic personage on their last walk. Saint Thomas More, Queen Anne Boleyn, Queen Katherine Howard, Lady Jane Grey, the Earl of Essex (in 1601), James Duke of Monmouth; the melancholy list is endless. Princess Elizabeth, later to be Queen Elizabeth I, walked through the conveniently secluded Traitor's Gate during the reign of her sister Mary. She was lucky to leave the Tower alive.

The Tower has been the scene of imprisonment within living memory. Hitler's deputy Rudolph Hess was kept here for a time, and others who were arraigned for espionage have been immured there to await trial. Eleven spies were shot at the rifle range during the First World War.

William's White Tower was built
to keep Londoners in check. A
heavy square keep with walls over
4 metres (13 feet) thick and some
28 metres (92 feet) high, it was
surrounded by a moat and later
protected by the addition of a
concentric defence plan with
curtain walls, flanking towers
surrounding the inner ward, and a
second outer wall punctuated by
riverside towers, and large bastions
on the landward side, with a ditch
encircling the entire mass.

The Tower complex has during
its long history been used as royal
residence, fortress, prison; has
housed a menagerie, the Public
Records Office, the Royal
Observatory and was for many
years an arsenal. Today it still has
an armoury that contains some of
the finest collections of weapons
dating from the days of Henry VIII.

The Tower was opened to the
public in 1875, and is one of the
main historic (and tourist) sights of
London. Its ravens strut the Tower
Green and the parade ground as
they did 500 years ago. The Crown
Jewels are guarded here, Beefeaters
are still posted at the gates, and the
Norman Chapel in the White Tower
is still a place of pilgrimage.

Tintagel
The ruins of a great castle stand on
one of the wild, windblown
headlands on the shore of
north-west Cornwall, a promontory
almost severed from the mainland
by the erosion of sea and rain. The
castle itself was built in 1145 by
Richard, Earl of Cornwall, bastard
son of Henry I. But the fame of
Tintagel does not spring from its
castle alone, but from a far more
ancient association. Under
Richard's grey castle lie the stones
of a monastery that was founded
about A.D. 500 and abandoned some
five hundred years later.

If the stories of Arthur,
half-legendary king of Britain who is
represented as having united the
British Isles against invading
barbarians have any substance at
all, and there is a mass of English
literature to support the theory,
then it is not surprising that this
antique site claims to be Camelot,

The Tower of London on the bank of the
Thames, still garrisoned after almost a
thousand years of constant use.

the Court of King Arthur and his Knights of the Round Table. Parts of the monastery fabric – it would have undoubtedly been a fortified complex used as castle and community house – may still be seen, a window here, a wall there, to lend veracity to the old, magical tales of Arthur.

Sir Thomas Malory, the English writer of the 15th century, whose book *Morte d'Arthur* is a main source of Arthurian information, relates that King Uther Pendragon, king of all England, summoned the Duke of Cornwall (of Tintagel, says Malory) in to his presence with his attractive wife, Igraine. Uther falls in love with Igraine. She will have none of it and departs with spouse to their stronghold at Tintagel.

Uther became wonderfully wroth, says the writer. The Duke, rather illogically, places his wife in the Castle of Tintagel and himself in his other castle, Terrabil. Uther

arrives with an army, 'laid a siege about Terrabil . . . and much people slain.'

Merlin, Britain's resident magician, came to the rescue. He clad Uther in the likeness of the Duke, infiltrated him into Tintagel and to Igraine's chamber, where 'Uther begat on her that night Arthur' – no doubt to the sound of rending heavens. Arthur was to become one of the mainstays of English folklore and legend, despite having started his existence under a cloud of deception.

Those who cannot bring themselves to believe in Tintagel's 1,500 years-old story may be forgiven, but the site and the stones are undeniably very old indeed, and Arthur's legends are so deeply entrenched in the histories of Brittany, Wales, Cornwall, the North of England and the lowlands of Scotland – all places where the old Cymri settled, driven thence by the Saxon invaders – that even by the 12th century, the date of Tintagel Castle itself, fascinating reports of King Arthur, his gentle knights and the quest of the Holy Grail were part of medieval literature.

Wales

The number of castles in Wales alone is the strongest evidence that such fortifications were very much part of local life in the Middle Ages. No less than 420 sites have been recorded in the small country and the figure does not include known castles that have since vanished.

Rarely were they planned for truly strategic reasons. Even those along the Welsh marshes that may appear to have been built to subdue the troublesome Welsh, were, in fact, usually constructed to extend their own individual lords' authority over his territory, and served coincidentally to delineate the boundaries of English property and influence, rather than to represent a coherent plan to defend the nation against the raiding Welsh.

Exceptions to this parochial aspect were of course the great Edwardian fortresses in Wales – Caernarvon, Conwy, Harlech, Beaumaris and others, part of the pattern of total authority of a king who was determined to keep a firm grip on Wales and its mercurial inhabitants.

Alnwick Castle, seat of the Percy family since the 14th century, was founded in about 1100 and fortified later in the 12th century.

Wales, a title designed to cement more firmly the union between Wales and England.

Caernarvon later withstood several sieges by the turbulent Welsh, who never succeeded in their case for independence. The castle opened its doors to history once more in modern times. Here Charles, first born son of Queen Elizabeth II, was invested Prince of Wales in 1969, the 21st of that title.

Conwy

Conwy (once spelt Conway) Castle was begun by Edward at the same time as Caernarvon although it was completed much more rapidly, in about eight years. Also standing on a narrow rock on the water's edge it was built on the century-earlier 'Château Gaillard' principle of

Above: Caernarvon Castle was built to guard the south-west end of the Menai Strait; Beaumaris held the northern end. This is Caernarvon's Eagle Tower at night.

Right: The north face of Caernarvon showing the King's Gate. This entrance was equipped with six portcullises, five doors and sundry murder holes.

Caernarvon

Edward I built Caernarvon Castle to secure the south-west end of the Menai Strait in North Wales, and to complement Beaumaris, which controlled the north from Anglesey. Like his other castles, it was a part of a fortress-and-fortified-town complex. It is a matchless example of a feudal structure, its plan determined by the shape of its rocky base, a wasp-waisted stronghold guarded by extensive curtains and polygonal towers, intended as the seat of government in the north and as a barrier against invasion by sea. It took over forty years to build, from 1283 to about 1330.

The people of Wales wanted a prince of their own. Their old continuous line of native princes had gone, the last, Llewelyn, in 1282. In 1284, King Edward held out his new first-born son to the crowds at the gates of Caernarvon Castle, suggesting that they might vow fealty to a prince who was born in their country, and who did not speak the English tongue. They eagerly agreed, and the new child, the first of thirteen that Edward's wife Eleanor of Castile presented to him, became the first Prince of

Above: The upper and lower wards of Caernarvon Castle, a strategically-sited fortress built between 1283 and about 1330.

Left: This view of Harlech Castle gives a false impression of its original siting: over the centuries the sea has receded from its walls.

putting up a series of obstacles to an enemy's progress, rather than constructing a formal concentric defence pattern which would not in any case, have been possible on this strip of land. It too was integral with the town, an Edwardian ploy for survival in the event of the town being besieged from the landward side, when supplies would be brought in to the defenders of town and castle by a sea route.

Harlech
The construction of Harlech Castle lower down on the west coast of Wales, and equally impressive in design and dramatic siting on a high rocky plateau, was also commenced by the energetic Edward I in 1283, and was brilliantly designed so that

it could be defended efficiently by a tiny garrison of some forty men who could like Conwy, be supplied by sea if necessary.

Built to a roughly quadrangular plan with a massive gatehouse in one wall, Harlech was a highly sophisticated defence-post. It took a thousand determined men to re-capture it in the early 15th century, when Owen Glyndwr had besieged and taken it for the Welsh. Some of the enormous stone cannonballs that are still at the castle illustrate the severity of the battle. During the 17th century Harlech was shuttled between Royalist and Parliamentary forces and stood siege for a year with a garrison of just twenty-eight men.

Conwy Castle, also built by Edward I, was completed in eight years (1283–89). Its 'linear' design is similar to Caernarvon.

Harlech, some 25 miles south-east of Caernarvon, was built to a roughly square plan with concentric defences (1283–90).

The Norman Keep on its raised motte is the main surviving historic feature of Cardiff Castle.

Cardiff

The Romans had found much the same difficulty in occupying Wales as did the English. North-south mountain ridges can be a formidable barrier to any who wish to travel east-west and when the natives object such movement is almost impossible. However, the Romans built several castles and stations in the country, among which was Cardiff Castle. Today its Norman keep is its main feature, and just a few courses of Roman masonry show through in its outer walls. Cardiff Castle still plays an active and frequent part in the city's life. Its banqueting hall is used for marriage feasts and its bailey is still the scene of many a tournament – gentler now than of yore, though showjumping can be a highly competitive contest . . .

Castell Coch

Another small castle some ten miles north of the capital of Wales is Castell Coch, the Red Castle. Nestling into the side of a tree-clad hill, its command of the approaches from the sea gave it supreme authority in this region during the 13th and 14th centuries. It was restored during the Romantic period by the Marquis of Bute and today is the only example in Britain of a perfectly reconstructed castle in the continental style – even to the conical roofs that adorn its towers. Its interior also claims interest – a beautifully restored medieval home that has a tremendous aura of authenticity, though completed in the 19th century. Its ravens are said to guard a great treasure buried in the grounds. It has never been found.

Scotland

When Edward I turned from his castle building in Wales to re-establish his position in Scotland, he found that the Scots themselves knew something about castle building. The English king, during a fighting campaign that took him as far north as Elgin, experienced several hard cold sieges on his way. Earlier Norman speculators who had their acquisitive eye on England's bellicose northern neighbour had left their calling-cards in the shape of numbers of motte-and-bailey establishments in the lowlands, some of which had been developed into menacing stone fortresses. Further north, many castles and towers had been established by the great Scottish families who were constantly warring against each other, either in their own or in the King's name. In the 17th century embellishments were made to many of them in the French-châteaux style – wings, turrets, castellations and corbels eventually eclipsing the main body of the castle. The resulting style became known as Scottish baronial.

Edinburgh

The massive rock that dominates the city of Edinburgh has undoubtedly been a fortified position since the dawn of civilization. Rebuilt in the 7th century by Edwin, King of Northumbria, the castle was used as a royal residence in the 11th and 12th centuries. Surrendered to Edward Plantagenet's great-grandfather, Henry II, the forces of Edward I also occupied it, the English monarch himself having died in Cumberland on the march. Much later, in 1650, Cromwell besieged and took Edinburgh Castle – but not by force of arms alone. Not until he threatened to blow up the entire rock with explosives, and with it no doubt a fair portion of the city, did the garrison surrender. In the 17th century the castle was again besieged, by the forces of William of Orange, who was at this time chasing out the adherents of his father-in-law, King James II, who had fled to France when his subjects had finally tired of his tyranny and had invited the representative of the House of Orange, and his wife Mary, to assume the monarchy.

Edinburgh Castle is still garrisoned, and still marks the time of day by a gunfire salute which thunders across the city at one o'clock.

Dunderave

Built in 1596 by the reigning chief of the Clan Macnaughton, and restored in the early part of this century, Dunderave Castle is in a lovely setting on the edges of Loch Fyne. In 1627 Alexander Macnaughton sailed to France with two hundred men from his property to aid the Stuart cause, a service which earned him a knighthood after the Restoration.

Craigievar

Completed in 1626, Craigievar Castle in historic Aberdeenshire has been continually occupied since then. The tower was originally surrounded by a barmkin wall enclosing a courtyard in which the kitchen and stables were

Dunderave Castle, built for the chief of the Clan Macnaughton in 1596. This idyllic castle was restored in the early part of this century.

Above: Nestling into the side of a tree-clad hill north of the Welsh capital is Castell Coch, a 13th century stronghold restored to past perfection 600 years later.

Right: Glamis Castle. The Old Pretender James Francis Edward Stuart, was entertained in the magnificent castle of Glamis during the 1715 Jacobite rebellion, and Mary Queen of Scots rested and dined there on her famous journey north in 1562 to quell Huntley's rebellion. The home of the Lyons family since 1372, Princess Margaret was born at Glamis in 1930.

Above: Edinburgh's ancient castle stands on a crag that overlooks the Scottish capital city, still a grim fortress, still garrisoned.

The drawing room at Glamis Castle, home of Britain's Queen Mother, some 12 miles north of Dundee.

Balmoral Castle. Originally a 16th century tower belonging to the Gordons, Prince Albert, Queen Victoria's Prince Consort had it rebuilt during the 19th century of white Crathie granite in the Scottish Baronial style. Beautifully situated on a curve of the River Dee at the foot of Craig Gowan, it is the Sovereign's Scottish residence, used by the Royal Family as a holiday estate.

Craigievar Castle in Aberdeenshire. Begun in the 17th century by John Mortimer, the castle was completed by William Forbes about 1620 and today looks much as it did when it was newly finished. The entrance seen here is the only one to the castle.

The Great Hall of Craigievar Castle showing the screen across one end of the piper's gallery in the corner. An inscription over the fireplace says: 'Doe not vaiken sleiping dogs'.

accommodated. A portion of the wall remains on the west side. Craigievar, with its pinky-white walls and silver-grey roofs, is incomparably lovely, and legend has it that a ghost sometimes wanders through the rooms, silently opening and closing the doors.

Cawdor
Medieval Cawdor Castle, in the historic county of Nairnshire, picturesquely stands on rock at the top of a steep escarpment above the burn. On the east side it is protected by a dry moat across which a drawbridge leads to the main courtyard of the keep. The old tower, built in 1442–1468 by William, Thane of Cawdor, is surrounded by 16th century buildings, but it still retains the characteristics of a Scottish baronial fortalice when a baron ruled his vassals with undisputed power.

Glamis
A fine example of Scottish baronial architecture, Glamis Castle in Tayside (previously Angus) goes back a thousand years in history, the site having been once that of a favourite royal hunting lodge where Malcolm II died in 1033 after receiving a mortal wound from an assassin. Not unnaturally, Shakespeare used Glamis as a setting for the murder of Duncan by Macbeth, Thane of Cawdor and Glamis. Since the 14th century the castle has been in the possession of the Lyons family, later Earls of Strathmore and Kinghorne and forebears of Queen Elizabeth the Queen Mother.

After Lady Glamis was burnt at the stake in 1537 for supposedly conspiring to poison James V, the castle was forfeited to the Crown, but was restored to her son when her innocence was later established.

The central tower was built in the 15th century on the foundations of the old one, and the extensive embellishments added in the 17th century. The castle is reputed to have a secret chamber known only, says Sir Walter Scott, to 'three persons at once, the earl, his heir-apparent, and any third person they may take into confidence'.

The east façade of Cawdor Castle from the dry moat, showing the central tower. The keep was built by William, Thane of Cawdor in 1454.

37

Ireland

Blarney

The Irish, it was said, were not comfortable in large and spreading dwellings, whether fortified or not. And indeed many of the castles of that country seem to be small single units, often just a tower with a deeply recessed entry, its main defence a lack of apertures until the walls were well above escalading height.

Such a castle is Blarney, in County Cork, a castle whose name has passed into the English language. 'Smooth flattering speech', says the dictionary of the word blarney, 'cajolery, to flatter with a silver tongue'. The stone that is said to impart the silver tongue upon osculatory contact is still there set high in the tower wall built by the MacCarthys of Muskerry in the 15th century. The difficulty is that one has to lie on one's back and lean upside-down over the edge of the parapet to kiss it, a somewhat daunting procedure.

The origin of the legend is ascribed to a remark of Elizabeth I. When tired of the everlasting promises of Cormac Dermot MacCarthy, Lord of Blarney, to submit to the Crown, a promise he never fulfilled, she is said to have retorted: 'Blarney again, I will hear no more of this Blarney!'

This castle stands on a clearing some five miles from the city of Cork, still erect though a little worn with time and tourists. It had survived several civil conflicts, though its lord lost it to the Cromwellians through unwisely backing the losing Royalist faction.

Trim

Trim in County Meath was one of the numerous Norman motte-and-bailey castles to be built in that country after the Conquest. On rising ground above the River Boyne, it was at the time so far advanced in defensive concept that the local Irish had no knowledge of its technical weaknesses. However, they had courage and numbers, and before Trim Castle was a year old, they had forced its Norman keepers to withdraw, destroying it as they left.

The present castle was rebuilt at the beginning of the 13th century by Walter de Lacy, Lord of Meath, but when his master, King John, brother of Richard I, came to Trim Castle, his written communications were addressed as from the meadows outside the castle, suggesting that it was either still being completed or still too small to accommodate his large court. The castle we see today has a massive rectangle of walls with D-towers protecting a square keep of heavy proportions, the largest defensive construction the Normans ever built in Ireland. Recent excavations here have revealed some fine 12th century artefacts, both ornamental and domestic.

Above left: Blarney Castle, built in the 15th century – and on a bus route just 5 miles from Cork in Ireland. Famed for the stone said to impart the silver tongue.

Left: Trim Castle in County Meath, north of Dublin. Built by de Lacy, it was the temporary home of Prince Hal, later Henry V.

Châteaux of France

Chinon

On the bank of the Vienne, a river which rises in the Massif Central and joins the Loire near Saumur, a complex of three châteaux combine to form a single entity. Chinon's triune château is of the time of the bastion, the meutrière and archière, much more attuned to the science of war than its more decorative neighbour up-river.

Religion, war, sensuality and cruelty are the warp and weft of Chinon history. Here Henry II of England stayed when he hunted in Chinon's forest and it was here in 1189 that he died, bereft of friends. It was the scene of the imprisonment of 140 Knights Templar before they were viciously executed, and the venue of the burning of a large number of the Jewish populace for allegedly poisoning the water supply. Joan of Arc first met France's King Charles VII here on 8th March 1429, when she urged him to march against the invading English. Her campaign roused the fervour of both the nobility and the French people, and the English were forced slowly out of France as a direct consequence of that first meeting at Chinon. The spring evening on which Joan met the Dauphin was described thus by a writer of the day: 'The inhabitants of Chinon received her with enthusiasm as the purpose of her mission had preceded her . . . she was received by the King in the Grande Salle, lighted by fifty torches and containing three hundred persons. The seigneurs were all clad in magnificent robes, but the king, on the contrary, was dressed most simply. The Maid advanced towards him without hesitation, "Dieu vous donne bonne vie, gentil roi," said she . . .'

The lazy, pleasure-loving young

The great three-castle complex at Chinon. Seen here are the Château du Coudray (left) and the Château du Milieu.

Chaumont, home of Diane de Poitiers, Catharine de Medici, and several cardinals of France, lies partly hidden above the Loire some 18 kilometres from Blois.

Dauphin – he was twenty-six years old and although king was as yet uncrowned – had spent much of his time idling here at Chinon and was reluctant to leave the caresses of his favourite mistress and his court entertainment to listen to a seventeen-year-old girl who had come to tell him of the desperate state of France. But such was her magnetic character that he acted upon her advice, giving her a suit of armour, a banner and an army, and followed her into battle. Joan stayed at Chinon more than a month and lodged in the Tour de Coudray, the older, most westerly part of the straggling riverside fortress.

Charles's son, later to be Louis XI, was educated at Chinon, the Prince of Conde, the distinguished Huguenot, lived here, and for a time France's eminence grise, Cardinal Richelieu owned it.

Chaumont

The château of Chaumont had its origins in the 10th century when the Counts of Blois owned it. They were succeeded by Cardinal Georges d'Amboise, predecessor of Richelieu, and Mazarin, as minister to Louis XII. In 1559, less than an hour after the accidental wounding of Henri II of France during a tournament, his wife Catherine de Medici sent a messenger to her arch-competitor for his love, the ageing but still beautiful Diane de Poitiers, who had heard of the accident and was weeping alone at Chenonceau. The widowed queen demanded, perhaps not unreasonably, the return of the Crown Jewels which the king had somewhat inconsiderately given de Poitiers, and that she vacate Chenonceau in Touraine.

'Is the king dead yet?' asked

Diane. The messenger replied, 'No, Madame, but his wound is mortal: he will not live the day.'

'Tell the queen then,' returned Diane, 'that her reign is not yet come, and that I am mistress still over her!'

But the seductress Diane soon had to leave the elegant château at the village of Chenonceau and move into the less comfortable Chaumont, the castle high above the broad sandy Loire, sometimes known as 'the fairest feudal castle in France' – a reference to its imposing façade. The deposed Diane little appreciated this and soon retired to her own château of Anet, near Dreux, closer to Paris.

Catherine had lived there for a time before giving it to Diane and being of a superstitious nature, had her astrologer Ruggieri close at hand. So close in fact that their bedrooms adjoined. 'There is a door opening from his room,' says a 19th century writer, 'which gives entrance to the winding stone staircase that leads to the tower top. Up this staircase the queen and the astrologer often went, that they might study the heavens together.'

Chaumont then passed through several hands, during the course of which it was visited by Voltaire and Flaubert, Georges Sand and other celebrated writers who lived a peripatetic life in search of copy. When a rich sugar merchant saw Chaumont in 1875, his spoilt daughter insisted that he bought it. He did, and she married a prince.

The young couple eagerly set to renovating the interior and giving the façade a face-lift. Its white towers with their blue slate conical roofs, its deeply recessed main door guarded by its pont-levis, its dignified rectangular cour d'honneur, with its fine views over the river below must have made a magnificent playground for its new occupants. Inside, Renaissance décor overlays most of the earlier work, and ornate salles for various social purposes abound.

Crossing the drawbridge (which by the way, is still operational, being pulled up for an hour or so during the staff lunchtime) one sees the cardinal's hat, the arms of the Amboise family, the initials of Louis XII and Anne of Brittany, and numbers of other somewhat mysterious cabalistic signs carved into the walls below the machicolations.

But, for all the noble owners of this castle, little of great nationally historic import took place there, and the air of perpetual tranquility is evident today as one strolls through the long inclined drive to the great lawns, and the firs that shield the castle from the east winds that often sweep through this low-lying region of the Loire.

Amboise

Between Blois and Tours on the south bank of the Loire the Château of Amboise spreads over a long spur of land. Amboise, one of the principal royal homes of the 15th and 16th centuries, housed most of the historic characters of those turbulent times, including the much-travelled 'Father of the French Renaissance' Francis I, and of course the iniquitous Italian-born Catharine de Medici (called Medicis by the French) and her retinue of voluptuous female spies.

The château, facing one of the shallow islands of this part of the

The river façade of Chaumont, with its girdle of small houses at the edge of the Loire.

river, has been part of this ancient town since around A.D. 496 when Christianity was established in the region. France's Charles VII lived here, and his grandson Charles VIII, who was passionately interested in architecture and rebuilt much of it. He erected the delicate Gothic Chapel, dedicated to Saint Hubert, the huntsman's saint, and with his queen, Anne of Brittany, built new apartments for himself and for his noble visitors. His plan was ingenious – a tower leading from river-level up to the hilltop living-quarters incorporated an immense spiral ramp (escalier de carosse) up which horses and carriages could be driven. The result was a kind of horse-age motel within the château, whereby guests could park their carriages immediately outside the doors of their own apartments.

It was through his interest in the reconstructions at Amboise that Charles came to a sad end. So eager was he to supervise his workmen, that he would oversee their labours at close range. Walking through a newly-constructed part one morning he struck his head on the lintel of a low doorway. He assured his companions that he was not hurt, but within the hour, collapsed. He died that night. The lethal lintel is still there.

The château of Amboise was the venue of one of the bloodiest scenes in the history of France when Queen Catherine de Medici forced her son Francis II and his young wife, the winsome Mary Stuart, Queen of Scots, and their ladies in waiting, all

Above: Between Blois and Tours on the south bank of the Loire, the Château of Amboise has been the home of several kings and has witnessed much of France's history.

Right: The pearl of the Loire châteaux, Chenonceau spans the river Cher in Touraine.

of them in full court dress, to witness the savage mass execution of Huguenot rebels after a conspiracy against the ruling families of the land had been discovered. Catherine insisted that the trembling young king and his wife, both of whom were speechless with horror, remain on their balcony while a scene of unparalleled butchery took place. Some 1,200 Huguenots were led to the axe: all sang a favourite psalm in unison. As the heads fell one by one the singing grew fainter, but the psalm continued to be heard until the last prisoner's turn came to die. Most of their bodies were thrown into the Loire but some corpses were hung on the castle walls. This scene haunted Mary, it is said, until her own day on the block.

After the Medici massacre, nobody was over-keen to call Amboise a home and for over two centuries it was used as a state prison mainly for notables who had fallen foul of the State. Later it was given to the Citizen-King, Louis Philippe (1773–1850) and today it belongs to the people of France.

A footnote that is perhaps as significant as any drama that occurred at Amboise during its long history is the fact that in 1515 Francis I persuaded Leonardo da

Vinci to leave Italy and live in the town, bringing with him his unique talents. His small manor-house on the other side of the town is now as important a pilgrimage as the château in which his bones are said to lie.

Chenonceau

Of all the châteaux de plaisance of France, Chenonceau on the banks of the Cher in Touraine, is the pearl. Lustred by the warmth of human habitation, and by the love and laughter and tragedy that history decreed it should see, its graceful splendour prompted France's Henri II to say: 'The castle of Chenonceau is the best and most beautiful in our Kingdom!' Chenonceau, spanning the river, seems still to echo the life of the 16th century, and its gardens still to bloom to the wishes of the beautiful Diane de Poitiers.

Once on this site stood a fortified medieval mill. Situated on the north bank, it had a small moat to protect it from marauders, behind which it peacefully ground the grain brought to its stone by boat and mule. Its owners, the Marques family, made a fatal error when they supported the Burgundians against the Dauphin in about 1420, allowing an English force to use their small fortress, and were thrown out when the tide of war turned.

The mayor of Tours, one Thomas Bohier, bought the mill and demolished the small building, leaving only a single keep tower, which can still be seen, a solitary sentry at attention in front of the entrance to the château. On the foundations of the old mill, Bohier erected his château, a small compact building on the side of the river.

The Bohier fortunes also waned and he was forced to relinquish the castle to the treasury of Francis I, King of France, successor of Louis XII. When Francis met his end in 1547, his son Henri II, husband of the ambitious Catherine de Medici (wife of one king and mother of three) inherited Chenonceau.

But he gave it to his paramour, Diane de Poitiers, the Court's great beauty of the age – who had played the same amatorial role with Francis, his father. It was Diane who added the five-arched bridge that spans the river.

Above: St. Hubert's Chapel, dedicated to the patron saint of huntsmen, crowns the château at Amboise, a gem of full-blown Gothic restored by Louis Phillipe.

When after Henri died, Catherine reclaimed Chenonceau she set about building a three-storey extension, the lower floor of which was a beamed gallery running the full width of the river over Diane's bridge, and spent much of her time there, often in the pleasant company of Mary Stuart, who was then Queen of France.

Under the direction of Catherine, fêtes and water-masques took place in this jewel-like château, including orgies of transvestism in which, as an English visitor wrote after a confusing evening in the long gallery, 'Nobody rightly knew which they had seen, a woman as king or man dressed as queen.' He added that 'the ladies were half naked with their hair down as if they were brides'.

Chenonceau's long gallery may still be walked today, although the visit will be cultural rather than Bacchanalian. The gallery was used as a hospital in the First World War and became part of an escape route in the following conflict. The north shore of the river was for a time in Occupied France and the opposite side of the river – and of the long gallery – on the 'Free' French side. Several desperate escapees made the dash to freedom there, sprinting down the length of the 60-metre room to add another chapter to the story of Chenonceau.

Azay-le-Rideau

From Orleans to Angers the banks of the long shallow Loire valley shelter many a celebrated château, varying in style from feudal to Renaissance.

When the French Court under the Valois found that the region had such an agreeable climate and topography, the Court nobility began to leave their palaces in Paris and spent most of their leisure time there. 'Touraine is the most delicious and the most agreeable province of the kingdom. It has been named the garden of France for the softness of its climate, the affability of its people, and the ease of its life,' said a contemporary scribe.

The great castle-palaces, some of them older buildings covered with Renaissance icing, others built after the spread of the Renaissance, lie at peace now on the water's edge of the great Loire, the Cher, the Indre and the Vienne, still as sharp and clean as they were when Francis I had his armorial Salamander carved above the portcullis.

'If the vast Chambord is the most impressive of the Loire châteaux, then Azay-le-Rideau must certainly be called the most elegant,' said Balzac. Basking in a pool fed by the Indre on the edge of the Chinon Forest, surrounded by greenery and silence, Azay-le-Rideau is undoubtedly one of the finest pieces of French Renaissance of the early 16th century. Mirrored permanently in its glassy pond, this château, feminine to its foundation-garment of local stone, wears its mock machicolations, its token-defensive bartizan turrets, like a woman's accessories.

It is not surprising then to learn that a woman caused it to be built, her name, Phillipe Lesbahy, wife of Gilles Berthelot, mayor of Tours and treasury financier to Francis I. Phillipe had inherited the ruins of a former castle on the site and even though its macabre history (a century earlier, in 1418, the Dauphin of France had massacred over three hundred of its residents and had dismantled the château) might have deterred a more squeamish girl, she decided to set up a new home there.

Permission to fortify Azay had been granted, and although fashion decreed that any fortified features should be for embellishment only, some sort of solid defence was useful in the area at a time when diverse 'public thieves, bad lads, and other types of vagabonds' would pay unwelcome visits before retiring with their loot into the dark Chinon forests.

Berthelot, typically, it would

Left: A view of Chenonceau from its gardens shows the Marques Tower (left), the last relic there of feudal times when a fortified mill occupied the site.

Right: Azay-le-Rideau has lain dreaming in its green pool, fed by the lazy river Indre, since the early 16th century. On the edge of the Chinon Forest, it is the most tranquil of the Châteaux of Touraine.

Preceding page: Magnificent Chambord, the breathtaking château in the Solonge near Blois, was built by France's King Francis I as a hunting lodge.

Right: Chambord's 'double-spiral' stairway. Reputedly designed by Leonardo da Vinci, it allows one to ascend without meeting anyone who may be descending it at the same time.

seem of Court financiers of the time, fell foul of his royal master almost as soon as he had got the château roof on, and fled. Francis also in character, gathered Azay-le-Rideau to his royal bosom.

Today one finds the arms of the pleasure-loving king and the ermine motif of his wife Claude of Brittany above the château entrance. Inside the château the rooms are exquisitely decorated with sculptured reliefs over the chimneys and ornate panels covering the stone walls. Portraits and paintings that are impressionist in principle if not in style, picture life in the 16th century and later. Anne of Austria shows off 'the fairest hand and arm in France'; Mary Stuart and the Maid of Orleans are there; Henri IV's paramour Gabrielle d'Estrées sits half-nude in the bath with her children, all finely recorded in oils.

If the legion of historic figures ever stepped down from their frames, half the nobility of medieval and Renaissance France would be there. Everywhere at Azay there is a rich, though not florid, display to delight the eye. 'And when one wanders through park following park, shaded by great forest trees, and here and there crossing the river on a picturesque bridge, catching almost at every turn some glimpse through the leaves of the white château, the blue turreted tops, the green lawn, the balustrade with its crimson vine . . . there is but one Azay-le-Rideau' said a Victorian visitor. Nothing has changed.

Chambord

No social convulsion has ever destroyed so many historic relics as the Revolution. Neither Cromwell's slighting of the churches and castles of Britain, nor two world wars, wreaked so much wanton damage as the French upon their own heritage.

The Château de Chambord, in the spreading forest bordering the sandy Sologne region through which typically French country roads run straight-as-a-die to reveal brief glimpses of the elephantine building, was no exception. During the Revolution it was gutted of its fine decorations and priceless furniture by the mob, and its external fabric heavily mutilated.

This vast folly started life modestly enough, as a small forest hunting lodge a few leagues south-east of Blois. But when Francis I, bored with his court at the Blaisois capital, saw the site in 1518, the Valois king decided that this was to be his own hunting lodge, which meant complete reconstruction.

What a reconstruction! A wall, 'the longest wall in France' was built enclosing some 13,000 acres around the new château. The building itself, with its 130-metre façade, its 440 rooms, its petrified forest of 365 chimneys and its seventy-four stairways is the largest Renaissance château in Europe, the French will claim. It seems a modest enough assertion, for a first sight of this château defies description – it appears to the newcomer so impossibly large, that the eye refuses to accept it as a concrete reality. It was designed precisely to take away the breath of visiting royalty, to dazzle with grandeur, to over-awe with sheer size.

At the same time, it had to be real and solid and practical enough for Francis. His family, court officers and nobility travelled in a cavalcade of some 1,200 horses and mules every one of which had to be accommodated at Chambord, in addition to his visitors. When the king died in 1547, the work of building continued under his son Henri II. Various architects and artists seem to have had a hand in the design and this probably accounts for its highly inconvenient interior. What further chaos would have resulted if Francis had implemented his original plan of diverting the Loire so that, as his chronicler wrote, 'the great palace could bathe its feet in the limpid waters of the river' one hesitates to contemplate. In the event, the smaller River Cosson was diverted to lap the stones, providing a pleasant river elevation.

It takes little imagination to envisage the gilded court of Francis I here at Chambord, brocaded and ermined nobles chatting and strolling about the balustraded terraces beneath the bell-towers and the ornate chimneys, the King of France occasionally casting a glance at his son Henri and daughter-in-law the young Catherine de Medici. Today the château is empty and echoing, but one can sometimes hear the sounds of the great days of Chambord.

The château itself is built on a cruciform plan enclosed in a mock defensive rectangle of wall and huge pot-like towers. Guard-rooms abound, and domestic quarters seem squeezed into corners to make room for the security personnel. In the centre of the building a double-helical staircase said to have been designed by Leonardo da Vinci, who certainly visited the château whilst living at Amboise, is Chambord's most notable internal feature. The two spirals are built intertwined enabling one to ascend the stairs without the necessity of meeting anyone who may be descending. It was said to have played quite a significant part in the scandals of the time. Francis spent a total of forty days in his self-acclaimed masterpiece, and indeed, although it was visited by monarchs and princes during the following years, it was never an official royal residence. The château now belongs to the nation, its land a 'Reserve National de Chasse' (a hunting area) exclusive to government members and guests.

Meung-Sur-Loire

On the north side of the fast-flowing river, Meung-Sur-Loire is a twisting, forgotten little place with its infant River Mauve flowing along numerous back-street channels to the main waters of the Loire.

Meung, ancient enough to have a Latin name, Magdunum, congenial enough to be the chosen home of Jean Ingres, a distinguished painter of the early 19th century, and historic enough to have a riverside quay called Jean d'Arc, boasts a church and monastery but hides its rather more historic château which was opened to the public for the first time in 1976. Few pilgrims penetrate beyond the pleasant square to visit the fortified building in which Joan lodged before her troops took the English-occupied town of Beauregency nearby.

A château de plaisance of the Bishops of Orleans for nearly six centuries, Meung has been reaping the harvest of neglect for the last two. Now privately owned, it rests in its quiet garden, its roofs moss-patterned, its paintwork peeling and its woodwork cracked – none of which dilapidations lessen in any way the soporific magnetism of the place. The visitor has the curious feeling that he has at last arrived at the destination he has long sought.

This small château has been more than once the scene of drama, violence and cruelty. The 12th century tower near the main gates was for many years the salle-des-questions and dungeon, and housed many a transgressor of civil or ecclesiastic law. Since the Bishops themselves were not allowed to shed blood in justice, they usually left their condemned prisoners in an oubliette under the tower dungeon, or on a narrow ledge halfway down the château well, from where they would conveniently make their exit without being subjected to judicial violence.

The château's most memorable prisoner was, perhaps, François Villon, poet and vagabond of the 15th century. He spent a summer in the dank rat-infested dungeon on a bread-and-water diet and this solitary life only came to an end when Louis XI visited Meung and marked the occasion with an amnesty.

The Maid of Orleans drove the English out of the town in 1429, lodging in the château with her forces. Local legend tells us that one morning the French troops garrisoned in the château witnessed the strange sight of a number of English officers of high rank hunting a fox in the distant countryside. One can imagine the incredulous delight of the French as the fox turned, headed straight for the hidden French lines, followed enthusiastically by hounds and riders . . .

Modern history has not passed by this secluded castle. Its last claim to a rôle in the history of France was not many years ago. Meung was used by the German High Command as its regional headquarters during the Second World War.

The Château of Meung-sur-Loire, a small town near Orleans. Here Joan of Arc rested with her troops in 1429 during the campaign against the English.

Sited on an ancient Roman river-crossing, Sully was the home of the young Charlemagne over a thousand years ago. It was rebuilt by a marshal of France in the early 17th century.

Sully

The Château de Sully sits amid drowsy carp some 20 kilometres north west of Gien, the town where Caesar crossed the Loire on his way northwards to Britain.

Sully's stronghold rests on piles driven deep down into the river bed by the Romans when they erected the earliest of the forts on this site to protect their newly-built bridge over the Loire. The castle was one of the first built in the region, and here Pepin, Prince of All the Franks, set up his court in A.D. 752. His wife Berthe-au-Grand Pied (a straight-from-the-shoulder description of her deformed foot) gave birth to a son, Charles who was to become the greatest ruler of his age, Charlemagne.

There had been Counts of Sully since the 12th century at this château at the gateway to Orleans but its most distinguished owner was undoubtedly Maximilien de Bethune, who acquired it in 1602. It had already taken part in an historic vignette in Joan of Arc's time, when the Tremoille family owned it. She had fought the English at Patay and raised the siege at Orleans, while her monarch Charles VII lurked behind the protective walls of Sully. Joan persuaded him to travel to Rheims, where he was crowned. However, he was later enticed back to the château by the wily owner who wished to influence the weak and shifty king. Joan of Arc followed and narrowly escaped being quietly thrown into the river by Georges de

La Tremoille – only to be captured by the English and burned.

Maximilien, a man of some energy and honesty, who was Superintendent of Buildings in France under Henri IV, rebuilt the château which had, with some 6,000 other castles and manors, been almost totally ruined during the Wars of Religion. He also rebuilt most of a country that had been devastated by war. Superintendant Maximilien was a great worker and his work earned him the title of Duc de Sully. He later applied his constructive talents to his own home, planning avenues of trees, moving the course of the river, and building a levee that can still be seen today.

Voltaire stayed at Sully after his dismissal from the court in 1716 and wrote his first drama there. A young girl of his own age – twenty-two – wanting to be an actress, seduced him and became his mistress. Voltaire unwisely allowed her to play a leading role in *Oedipe*. She was abysmal in the part, but she still managed to persuade the besotted Voltaire to write a part for her in his next play, also written at Sully, with similar results. They parted, but the affair that had started at the château haunted Voltaire all his life, and they met one final time shortly before he died, some sixty years later.

The château at Sully played a more recent role in the tumult of war. In 1940 the town and château were caught up in the German advance and when the liberating forces turned the tide, a fleet of American bombers dropped fifty tons of high explosive on the local bridges, severely damaging the château. It was restored in a remarkably short time and Sully lives again. Its towers and roofs are pristine and its interior one of the finest in France.

Fontainebleau

Fontainebleau's château, a sprawl of brick and stone under a maze of mansard roofs and dormer windows, is no fortress. Its gigantic horseshoe staircase at the main entrance dwarfs the access doors themselves but nevertheless is designed to invite rather than repel visitors.

Francis I of France had been taken hostage at the battle of Pavia

Above: The Fountain Courtyard at Fontainebleau.

Right: Fontainebleau's François I Gallery. Decorated for this energetic French king in about 1534 it has twelve huge frescoes surrounded by elaborate ornamentation.

in 1525. A year later he was returned to his native land and decided to set up a home or two in Paris. He built a château in the Bois de Boulogne, and rebuilt the old and well-worn château at Fontainebleau in the forest land a few leagues south of the capital itself. Francis had witnessed the Renaissance of painting and architecture during his Italian campaigns, and wished to encourage its spread to France. He hired an army of Italian sculptors and painters and craftsmen to refurbish Fontainebleau rather than to reconstruct it, for his wish was simply to rival in richness the interior of the Vatican and various Renaissance palazzi in Italy. His workers adorned the existing building with terra-cotta plaques, with busts, with frescoes and stuccos – no less than twelve huge frescoes appear in the Long Gallery – with sundry pediments and, to be fair, with some very fine

Renaissance windows. An inner ward was transmogrified into the Oval Court, and later, after the death of Francis, the famous White Horse Courtyard – the main entry to Fontainebleau – was constructed from what had been an old farmyard.

Some of Fontainebleau's main elevation dates from Francis and his initials can still be seen on the pilaster capitals, but much of the château was rebuilt and greatly extended during the following three centuries. The great horseshoe staircase was built in 1634 and is perhaps the most poignant relic of Napoleonic history here, for it was on these steps that on 20 April 1814, Napoleon bade an emotional farewell to his Guard before his departure for Elba.

Somehow the Revolution had left the château almost unscarred. The French Military Academy had taken it over in 1803; Napoleon turned them out, replacing the furnishings and décor with his own, planting the letter 'N' over most of the lintels and gates, weaving his self-styled emblem the bee (denoting energy and honest toil) into much of the linen and tapestries. He too avoided structural alterations on a large scale, merely re-planning rooms, creating a series of State apartments and a number of modest living quarters.

Although Fontainebleau was restored throughout by Louis Philippe in the 1830s the château is seen today much as Napoleon left it. Even the newlyweds that walk after their marriage ceremony to the château gardens for their wedding photographs seem to be part of Fontainebleau's continuing history.

Gaillard – the keep. 'I'd capture it even if its walls were made of iron,' said France's Philip Augustus – who fulfilled his promise in 1204.

Château Gaillard

The site of this late 12th century fortress at Les Andelys was carefully chosen to guard the approaches to Rouen. Although the spur which commands an enormous loop of the Seine on which Gaillard was built,

was some ten leagues (49 kilometres) from the capital of Normandy, the route that an advancing force would have to take on its journey from the region of Paris would, in the 13th century, be so densely forested that progress would be practical only along the river or its banks. Circumnavigating a castle so strategically placed would confront an army with a near-impossible task and they would have no alternative but to engage and subdue any stronghold in their narrow path.

Thus Gaillard, an immense work of solid stone dedicated to the defence of the English-held Norman city and situated between Paris and Rouen, a fortress that fitted into its green and rocky knoll in a way few medieval structures did, affected a camouflage comparable to the military art today.

Gaillard was built by England's Richard Coeur de Lion in 1197 to a plan that embodied all the progress made in design during the Norman period, a fortress designed by Richard himself using the knowledge he had gained fighting in the Levant. Richard was pleased with Château Gaillard; he called it his *Bellum Castellum de Rupe*, the fair castle of the rock.

Richard had returned to England after several years absence on the Third Crusade and a hazardous journey home after shipwreck, capture and imprisonment, to find that his brother John had been stirring up revolt against him. He generously forgave John and sailed for France to protect his remaining territorial possessions against the ravages of Philip Augustus, King of France.

Gaillard had double the conventional castle defences with a second, outer, ring of walls. These were punctuated closely and regularly by a series of flanking towers, designed to cover all dead ground at the approaches and near the walls of the castle. The plan of Gaillard is an elongated one, with three baileys in line, following the shape of the promontory. The keep faces the river, towering above a steep cliff of white rock, a natural barrier against attack. To reach the keep, an enemy would have had to penetrate through the towered walls of the first bailey, cross a moat to the second, demolish that, then breach

a heavy wall protecting the keep and the inner bailey. The walls of the keep were two metres thick and deemed impregnable.

Philip, stung by this show of strength, boasted that he could take Gaillard even if it had walls of iron. Richard retorted that he could hold it even if its walls were made of butter . . . but he was wrong.

After Richard's death at Chalus, Philip fulfilled his boast. The siege of Château Gaillard in 1204 was one of the most memorable in history. Partly due to one small and seemingly insignificant fault in design that allowed Philip's sappers to pick their way into the walls under cover of dead ground, the castle fell.

Philip's forces had gained access to the outer bailey early in the siege. Then luck entered the drama. A French soldier who had been prowling around the walls noticed that a shaft leading down from a garderobe opened near a window of Château Gaillard's chapel. He led a small party of Philip's men up this insalubrious shaft, into the chapel, setting up a tremendous clamour. The garrison panicked, fled to the inner bailey within the chemise that encircled the keep. Philip brought up his sappers, found the single 'dead' point under the last defence wall, dug into it, propped it with stout planks, set fire to the wood, and the last 'impregnable' defences of Gaillard tumbled down.

Pierrefonds

A cluster of houses, a small lake, a café or two are the basic ingredients of the village of Pierrefonds near Compiegne. Nestling in a hollow like the palm of a gigantic hand, the small community has for centuries grown its crops, kept its bees, and when at all possible, let the tide of history flow over its roof-tops. Its one claim to an historic footnote is its château. It dominates the village like a giant grey shadow. Its fantastic size and the sudden shock of its appearance as one rounds an unsuspecting country bend, would even make that genius of the fantastic, Walt Disney, gape in awe.

Product of the Romantic Revival of the 19th century, the present Château Pierrefonds, designed for Napoleon III, was built on the ruins of an earlier castle. It was intended as a home for the Bonaparte monarch and a grandiose setting for his court.

The history of Pierrefonds begins, as with so many towns and villages of France, in the 11th century. Philip Augustus acquired the forested lands a few leagues east of the Oise and a day's ride north of Paris, but the castle was not started until several generations later – by Louis d'Orleans, in about 1393, a work which was abandoned when he was murdered.

The Hundred Years War and the Wars of Religion saw the château attacked, besieged, taken, plundered and destroyed several times. In the 17th century it was captured by royal troops, and on Cardinal Richelieu's command demolished by mine and fire.

Napoleon III decided to restore the ruins to their former glory. Monsieur Violet le Duc, archaeologist and architect, was commissioned to carry out the gargantuan task of transforming the skeletal remains into an imperial residence. His renovation of France's Notre Dame Cathedral and other ancient buildings fitted him for this labour. His structural efforts produced a massive complex that was a fairly accurate copy of the ancient château, but his interior work, executed in the most solemn but fanciful Gothic manner, over-dignified and over-decorated, led to some criticism of what was termed the 19th century 'Troubador Style'. Later work on the castle produced so many completely new curtain walls, battlement and towers, that in effect Pierrefonds became more of a new château than a remodelling. Sometimes called the most unsympathetic restoration of the Romantic Period, Pierrefonds is nevertheless one of the architectural pilgrimages of Northern France.

Footnote: Clearly the design of the fairy castle in Disneyland was influenced by Pierrefonds. The towers with their deep machicolations, the sharp turrets and small windows, the drawbridge and entrance of the fascinating American castle are very similar indeed to the historic French château.

The massive bulk of Pierrefonds overshadows its small village. This giant castle near Compiegne started life in the 12th century, but was heavily restored in the 19th.

changed since the Breton Duke Jean de Rohan rebuilt the castle in about 1500, when new methods of warfare had rendered the old type of stronghold obsolete.

Earlier, Josselin had been one of the fortresses of a French 'line of strength' raised against the Bretons and their allies, owned by Olivier de Clisson, Constable of France and at one time the most distinguished of French knights who, the chronicle says, 'espoused Marguerite de Rohan, widow of Beaumanoir' a lady who had a reputation for beauty second to none.

De Clisson, the central historic figure of Josselin, had suffered a tragic childhood. His father, whose reputation was that of a hard and vengeful man, was accused of treachery to the State and had been guillotined in Paris.

Olivier acquired Josselin in 1370. It was he who enlarged it after it had been dismantled by order of the Dukes of Brittany, leaving much of the river-front with its tall towers untouched except for crowning the walls with roofs and dormers and widening arrow slits into windows. But he transformed the inner, landward, side of the château into one of the country's most delicately spectacular façades. Josselin's domestic side, hidden from public gaze, is a riot of balustrades and ogee windows and doors and carved decoration in the most playful of the French Flamboyant Gothic. This façade forms an astonishing

Above: The grim 14th century river-front of the château at Josselin on the Oust in Brittany.

Right: The Breton region's most formidable château, Josselin, seen from across its river-moat, the Oust.

The Château at Josselin

The grim stone towers and intimidating curtain walls reach from their great height down to the road that runs along the edge of the little River Oust at the small Breton town of Josselin. Old prints of the scene on display in the little half-timbered shops depict washer-women of the Fin de Siècle pounding their laundry in the chill waters, rippling the dark reflections of the château.

The scene has changed little since those days. Indeed it has hardly

contrast to the blank and military exterior, and is one of the classic examples of the evolving architecture of the early 16th century, and the transition from fortress to château.

Fougères

The château of Fougères on the eastern edge of Brittany is one of the most impressive examples of medieval feudal military architecture. Besieged by Henry II in 1166, it was destroyed, but like most important strongholds of the day, was rapidly rebuilt, in this case by its overlord, the celebrated Breton Baron Raoul II, although the town fell to the English on a number of other later occasions, the most notable one being in 1449, when the town forces were commanded by the Spanish renegade Surienne of Aragon.

Like its near neighbour Josselin, Fougères continued to be developed, and its defences were, in the course of time, augmented by a series of moat-like ponds that separated it from the town itself, with the River Nançon forced into forming a moat proper on the western sides of the château.

During the 14th century, some of its towers were heightened and equipped with machicolations against siege-warfare techniques, a defence that was soon to become anachronistic. Shortly afterwards, the château's two great towers of Raoul and Surienne were modified to the new-style artillery warfare, arrow slits becoming gunloops and tower-tops artillery platforms.

These D-shaped towers showing the heavy curved front of the 'D' to the invader, are striking examples of the early appreciation of the devastating power of the new gunpowder weapons, and were far ahead of their time in military sophistication. The story of 15th century Europe was, historians will state, the story of the firearm. Its growing effectiveness was the mainspring for the changes that occurred in the territorial boundaries of the western world and of many of the changes in the balance of political power.

On the eastern edge of Brittany, the town of Fougères is protected by its château, first besieged in 1166 by the Plantagenet King Henry II.

The château at Fougères miraculously survived these rapidly advancing methods of warfare during the turbulent 15th and 16th centuries, but was bombarded again in the 20th century, when damage was caused to the town and château in June 1944.

This formidable château provides a unique opportunity today to study a well-preserved and important feudal castle through the times of its changes and modifications, particularly from the 12th to 16th centuries.

Saumur

The Château of Saumur, commanding the River Loire and its bridge on the old north-south route through to the Sarthe region has been a stronghold since the time of the great fortress builder Fulk Nerra, an ogre who lived in the fold of the Millenium and who seemed to manage to destroy as many châteaux as he built during his raging career.

The watercourse at this point is full and fast flowing – swollen by the tributaries Indre, Cher and Vienne

The château of Saumur, secure on its hilltop above the Loire town, was remodelled during the 15th century, a palace built upon a fortress.

– forming an impregnable front to this castle which like most Loire châteaux had, until the 15th century, formed part of a chain of defensive-offensive strongpoints.

Only the layout and the bases of the old towers were kept by its remodeller, Louis I, in the 15th century, who used Saumur for his gentle pleasures. In contrast with some other fortified dwellings built at that time, Saumur was first a palace with a superimposed fortress

for the religious conflicts of France dictated that the bastions and other businesslike fortifications of Saumur were built for serious purposes.

It is obvious that the castle was built for decorative purposes. Its upper parts are elegant and graceful, embellished with weathercocks of gilt, with bell-turrets and conical roofs and pinnacles and exquisitely carved gable-windows. It is without a keep,

in the 16th century Saumur became a recognized Huguenot stronghold, capital of the 'Huguenot Pope' Duplessis-Mornay, who had been given the castle and guarantees of security by Henri IV (of France and Navarre) who had earlier fought for the Protestant Huguenot cause.

The castle was a State penitentiary during France's Empire period and later became an arsenal and barracks.

The town is famous for its Royal Cavalry School, housed in the château since Louis XV who owned numerous châteaux both formal and discreet, (the latter being used by a succession of ladies of the quality of Mesdames Pompadour and du Barry) generously donated it for the purpose. The school is still there, its distinguished Cadre Noir demonstrating French equestrian 'haute école' to students of equitation throughout the world. Its staff of officers-in-training took part in a valiant episode of the last war, when they prepared the defence of their school. The enemy was at the gates of Saumur and the school staff were ordered to halt the German forces over a 20-kilometre line with their pitifully small numbers. They held the line for two days and nights against enormously superior forces.

Today the Cadre Noir is part of the National Institute of Equitation and in addition to demonstrating the French classical style of equitation, Saumur holds regular courses for civilian riding instructors.

South West France

This is the land of medieval conflict and present peace, of rivers that drift silently through field and gorge, of small secret farms hidden in the folds of shallow valleys and old mills that have not been visited for a generation. From deep inland, westwards along the winding valley of the Dordogne, flows the dark river to join the Garonne at Bordeaux, its towns and riverside villages little changed since the Middle Ages. Today the village doctor may live in a 12th century cottage cut into the cliffside on the edge of the river, the postman dwell in a cottage that was built in the time of Charles VI and the children play football under the arcades of a market place erected by England's

Edward I. The saying 'Nothing moves in the Dordogne except the chickens and the river' is apt for a region that has an unchanging population, no great natural resources and few towns of major importance in an industrial age.

Chalus
England's Richard I had, by 1198, built his great Château Gaillard commanding the approaches to Rouen. In 1199 Richard led a punitive expedition south to Chalus Castle near Limoges, where one of his henchmen, Adomar of Limoges, had discovered, and taken illegal possession of, a number of gold ornaments, probably Gallo-Roman, which had been discovered in the immediate vicinity of the small castle above the Tardoire Valley. Unfortunately Richard had a strong streak of greed in his character and undoubtedly expected a willing conveyancing of this treasure. Viscount Adomar however refused to relinquish any of it, although he had earlier offered part of the find to Richard.

The Count bolted the door, wound up the pont-levis and began shooting. Richard, hero of the western world, valiant and skilful at arms, a Crusader who had fought and survived a score of battles, received a cross-bow bolt in the shoulder, and died shortly afterwards. This is what a contemporary scribe, Ralph of Coggeshall, wrote of one of the most ironic incidents in history, 'After dinner on the third evening, the king, unarmed except for a helmet, boldly approached the tower with his men . . . A certain soldier who had stood almost all day . . . in one of the crenellations of the tower, and had avoided harm by catching all the enemy spears and arrows on his shield, observed the besiegers closely, and suddenly drew his crossbow. He fired a bolt at the King, who cried out: the bolt struck him in the left shoulder near the vertebra of the neck, the wound curving down the left side, because the King had failed to stoop far enough down behind the squareshield which was carried in front of him.'

Richard drew out the shaft but left the metal head in the wound. His surgeon extracted it later, but

relying on its position of total authority on top of a hill, high above the Quai de Limoges. A coloured miniature in the Chantilly Book *Les Très Riches Heures* of the Duc de Berri shows the castle in its full 15th century glory, with its agricultural workers harvesting the sweet wine-grapes of Saumur, even then fashionable in England and the low countries.

Favourite residence of the Angevin princes and English kings,

his clumsy probing injured the king still further. The wound turned septic. On 17 April 1199, eleven days after he had been wounded in this trivial affray, King Richard Lionheart died. The castle of Chalus and its bowman had ended a reign and turned the flow of history.

Richard I of England, born at Oxford, third son of Henry II, was finally laid at Fontevrault Abbey near Saumur. His remains are still there, lying next to those of his mother Eleanor of Aquitaine, Isabel of Angouleme, wife of his brother Prince John – and Henry II his Plantagenet father.

Beynac

Beynac, a small village on the north shore of the dark green river and almost in the centre of the region, is dominated by its castle, standing on a sheer knife-edge cliff 250 metres above the watercourse. Its history

Left: Beynac, a small village on the banks of the River Dordogne, is dominated by a château dating from the 12th century.

dates from Richard Lionheart's time. Richard allowed his notorious lieutenant, Mercadier, to use it as a base for local terrorism, and earned retribution from Simon de Montfort (father of the founder of England's Parliament) who was then fighting heretics in the region. He burnt Beynac down.

Montfort

De Montfort also treated a castle a few leagues upriver with equally cavalier consideration. He razed the castle at the loop in the Dordogne called the Montfort Run (the name was a coincidence only) a position which gave considerable command over the river, and was consequently often the objective of warring factions: the fact that Montfort castle has been rebuilt five times since 1214, amply illustrates its strategic importance on the Dordogne.

Below: De Montfort castle was razed and rebuilt five times during the Middle Ages, an indication of its strategic importance on the River Dordogne.

Bonaguil

The great Bonaguil near Cahors was possibly the last fortified castle to be built in medieval France. It was built, by father and son, as a defence against the English, but was not completed until some years after the last English soldier had sailed away from France. Its protracted construction illustrates the fast-changing trends in defences as gunpowder became the deciding factor in warfare. Bonaguil's original design was intended as a defence against escalades. When Bringon, son of de Roquefeuil, first inherited the work, machicolations, moats and drawbridges were still *de rigueur*, but by the time he had begun the second stage of the construction the advance of firearms dictated that Bonaguil be equipped to cope with gun warfare. No such encounter ever materialized and Bonaguil travelled into the 20th century as a fine and almost intact, example of the last of the French medieval forts.

Château de Biron

The Château de Biron, some seven kilometres from the 'Bastide Anglaise' (English fortified town) of Montpazier between the valleys of the Lot and the Dordogne, is a 'harmonious juxtaposition of three

Built during the period of firearms development, Bonaguil, near Cahors, is one of the last French medieval forts.

different styles of architecture' as the curator will advise. Built on a butte, a prominent knoll, Biron is what one may imagine to be a typical genuine 'Troubador' castle, with its skyline-profile and winding, never-ending approach-road through deserted greenery. Passing from French to English hands – and back again – during what is termed *les troubles Anglo-Français*, Biron is a vast complex of stronghold, mansion and chapel, built by the Gontaut-Biron family, one of the most distinguished French nobility, but a family whose fortunes were never of the most happy. Its record includes several exiles, one or two imprisonments and an execution for treachery to the crown in 1602.

Today the chapel is often used by the local school for choir practice. Its haunting acoustics give the childish voices an echoing etherial quality.

Montpazier

Montpazier, founded by Edward I in 1284, just along the River Dropt from Biron, is always a pleasant surprise to the visitor. Nothing, it seems at first glance, has changed since the late Middle Ages, its fortified walls and ports surrounding a huddle of houses and a square in which children still play sheltered by the same covered market place and arcades that kept their ancestors dry five hundred years ago.

Rocamadour

Rocamadour, château-and-village, is another site known to pilgrims since the 12th century, when according to somewhat shaky tradition the body of the locally venerated Saint Amadour was discovered, wonderfully preserved, in a small chapel there. Even Henry II made a visit to this miraculous

The Château de Biron, one of the remote magical French castles of the early Middle Ages.

corpse, the shrine's fame naturally spreading during the following years as numerous other monarchs paid homage there. The whole site seems to be an act of faith; even the bishop's palace and chapel buildings cling to the sheer face of a cliff by faith, reached by steps that are often negotiated by the faithful on their knees. The shrine itself is surrounded by a group of chapels. From a small square here a tunnel leads to the castle above, perched on the sharp edge of what appears to be a perpendicular, if not concave, drop. Much of the château was rebuilt in the 19th century but the feat of construction is no less courageous for that. The battlements provide a vertiginous view of the gorge below, a spectacle for the clear-headed only.

Château de Montal

The Château de Montal has no pretensions to such antiquity as many of the medieval castles of the Dordogne and its neighbouring regions, although it is one of the most fascinating. Montal, built around 1530, could have been located on the Loire; it is in fact just a few kilometres east of Rocamadour, near Saint Céré, but its style is that of the Renaissance château so often seen in Touraine, though more mellowed in appearance due to the warmer colour of the stones and tiles brought from local quarries.

Built by a loving mother for a son who had left for the wars, the château was to be a coming-home present for Robert de Montal. He never saw this delightful gift for he was killed during one of the many battles in Northern Italy. His mother, the gentle Jeanne de Balsac d'Entraygues, widow of Anauray de Montal, was inconsolable. She blocked in the dormer window from which she planned to greet her returning son, and inscribed upon it the pathetic motto 'Plus d'espoir', (No more hope).

The later story of this sad château is bizarre. It was acquired after the Revolution by a speculator who sold the sculptures and other items of value to buyers as far away as

America. By 1908, when it became the property of a M. Fanaille, there was nothing but the shell left. Fanaille, however, was a man of some courage. He set out to re-purchase every item that had been dispersed, some of them a hundred years earlier. He succeeded, with two exceptions. Some of the best sculptures had been bought by the Louvre and were then housed in Paris, and a dormer window had been purchased by the Metropolitan Museum of New York. The determined M. Fanaille copied the window, which he installed during his detailed restoration, later giving the château to the State, whereupon the Louvre returned the sculptures

to their original site. The family still lives at the château.

Castelnau

Near the confluence of three rivers, the Dordogne, the Cère and the Bave, the red châteaufort of Castelnau rises on a commanding hill. The 12th century stronghold, with its typical three defence lines and circular keep, has all the usual features of pre-gunpowder mechanics and appurtenances.

Below: Castelnau, a 12th century fortress on the confluence of three rivers in the Quercy region.

Bottom: The melancholy Château de Montal, built by a mother in the 16th century for a son who never returned from the field of battle.

Above: Château life was not always on a large scale. Here a small and, even today, unknown château, complete with lookout tower, sleeps away the centuries on its own river bank in central France, a land that supported countless such fortified homes during the Middle Ages.

Left: The Château of Fenelon, a stronghold site since the 13th century, was rebuilt in the 15th and 17th centuries to include a manor house.

Castelnau was built and occupied by a family who were rivals of, and frequently warring with, the Counts of Turenne. When they were forced to become subjects of Turenne, Louis VIII eased their humiliation by issuing an edict that whoever lived at the château should pay a toll as a sign of submission – the toll to be one egg a year. For many years a solitary egg was transported on a four-oxen wagon with due pomp and ceremony to the County of Turenne.

Eventually Castelnau fell into disuse and finally ruin, but was partly restored during the last century by a successful opera singer, and now officially rates as the second most significant military château in France. It houses a fine collection of art works and religious treasures from the 14th and 15th centuries in rooms which once housed a garrison of some 1,500 men at arms and 150 horses.

Château de Fénelon

The Château de Fénelon commands the River Dordogne not far from the north-south road from Limoges to Cahors, an important route when Fénelon was an English fortress, which role it served until the end of the Hundred Years War. Inside its walls lies a stately 17th century house, a cour d'honneur, a small courtyard with cloisters on three sides, a 14th century chapel, and a small tower built in the 15th century and known locally as the Tour de Confiture (Jam Tower), an innocuous name given to its less-than-friendly role during a siege. It was used to pour boiling oil on attackers but when oil ran out on one occasion, it is said that boiling jam was used instead.

Castles of Belgium, Holland and Denmark

Belgium

Beersel

The park at Beersel, a village in Belgium's Brabant region, is easily overlooked by the casual traveller. But once inside the park the clock is turned back to feudal times. The path into the wooded grassland reveals a small lake, a moat, a deserted drawbridge, a silent red brick castle. Its pointed towers stand like firework-rockets on the edge of the green water, its buttressed curtain walls drop down sheer to the moat, perfectly reflected in the still surface. A spreading tree shades the small circular courtyard, the crumbling wall-walk atop the curtain waits forlornly for a footstep

The covered wall-walk and machicolations at Beersel.

and the covered galleries over the machicolations doze in the sun.

Beersel's 13th century knight's room, its armoury, refectory, hall and domestic rooms speak of its feudal past, and the renovations of the 17th century are hardly noticed in this evocative atmosphere. No furniture or décor interrupts the imagination here, and few tourists seem to have discovered this compact example of medieval military architecture, the only intact example in Belgium today.

Beersel was built to defend the region against forces from Flanders

On the edge of the village of Beersel, just south of Brussels, moated Beersel Castle is a compact example of medieval military design.

and Hainault who frequently passed by on their way to attack Brussels. Built by a seneschal of Brabant (whose daughter prudently married the Lord of Stalle, owner of the next castle, a league or two away) the castle survived local skirmishes but eventually it fell into disuse.

In the 19th century a cotton magnate bought the building and site – and demolished part of the castle to accommodate a mill. Fortunately, during the past fifty years Beersel has been painstakingly restored to its former state.

Vèves

'A handsome and strong stone-built château, with as many as six or seven towers defending its sides, situated on a rock . . .' Thus wrote a 17th century chronicler of this classic stronghold on the edge of the Belgian Ardennes. And the description holds good today. The castle is situated on an ideal strategic site commanding the valley of the Ry de Mirande below.

Vèves has an elusive, secretive air. Its hatted towers glower at the countryside, its windows seem to watch every movement in the village under the grey curtain walls. An eagle's nest from one side, half-hidden from passing view, a fortress from another, with a touch of the Scottish baronial when seen from its main gates, this castle fits into the wooded Ardennes as if it were placed there by nature herself.

The castle was built by an early Lord of Beaufort in the 12th century and its history has been bound up with the Beauforts, and later the Counts Liedekerke de Beaufort whose descendants lived there until as recently as 1977, when the present count gave Vèves Castle to the State.

Vèves has been restored over a long period. When the Renaissance arrived the castle 'hung up its crossbow on the wall, adorned its head with roofs, decked itself out with windows, cultivated its new garden – taking up civilian life with the grand martial airs of a half-pay officer.'

The rooms of this compact castle are a delight to the eye; most are fully furnished, with the stamp of Louis XIV and XV seen in the various styles.

A fascinating lady of English

Above: Galleries and timber structure at Vèves.

Far left: Vèves in Belgium's Ardennes. 'Ung beau et fort chasteau de pieres,' said a medieval chronicler. 'A fine strong stone castle.'

descent once lived at Vèves. Her name, Barbara Villiers, Duchess of Cleveland; her previous occupation, mistress of King Charles II of England. Of that liaison was born a girl, Charlotte Fitzroy, a direct forebear of the Countess Liedekerke de Beaufort.

Gravensteen

'This powerful fortress of Gravensteen (Château des Comtes, in Belgium's other language) inevitably produces a profound surprise for those who contemplate it for the first time. Great indeed is the contrast existing between the

Left: Gravensteen, or the Château des Comtes, in Ghent is a grim medieval fortress surrounded by bustling 20th century traffic.

Below: This lofty castle at Walzin near Dinant in Belgium was founded in the 13th century on a natural-defence site.

mass of grey stone surmounted by an enormous keep and the busy and narrow street which leads to it.'
This extract from the official history of the massive Castle of the Counts of Flanders evokes precisely the sense of shock one receives on the sudden appearance of this 12th century mass in the middle of bustling 20th century Ghent in East Flanders.

The date inscribed above its main entrance is 1180, indicating that Gravensteen is sited, as so often occurs, on the foundation of an even earlier fort dating back to the Roman occupation.

Gravensteen's grim looks do not belie its history. Outside its barbican, medieval justice was administered and savage sentences executed. A building in the forecourt was long used as a torture chamber, and until the 18th century the barbican itself was a prison.

Left: The central keep at Gravensteen. The Ghent fortress dates from the 9th century, was rebuilt in the 11th, and restored in the 19th.

Below: The best-known Dutch 'wasserburg' or water-castle is the brick-built Muiderslot, started about 1284.

square-planned, drum-towered stronghold with an exposed-bridge approach to its gate house. Built about 1284 by Count Floris IV of Holland, it is typical of the general

Belgium's 'Magna Carta' known as the Joyeuse Entrée (Joyous Entry) was enacted here in 1356, in which the Brabant dukes promised that they would extract only legal taxes from the populace, pledged not to declare war without the agreement of the burghers of Ghent – and gave subjects the right to revolt if the nobility exceeded their powers.

The castle was originally built to defend Ghent against outside attack. However, it appeared that many of the citizens of Ghent built houses so tall and solid that Gravensteen's 14th century overlord re-aligned his defences to repel possible attacks by the good burghers themselves 'so high were their houses that they might be taken for towers.'

Holland

The Muiderslot
During the Middle Ages the Low Countries comprised a number of small states or countries often separated – or joined – by waterways, an invariable pointer to the location of defence works in the region. All one has to do is look for the joins; there one finds the strongholds. Modern Holland still has some 200 to show in various states of repair, of the 2,000 that flourished in medieval times. Most are, naturally, of Wasserburg (water-castle) type, guarding canal approaches to towns or cultivated regions.

Best-known of Dutch castles is the brick-built Muiderslot at Muiden, near the Ijssel Meer, a style of castle-building in a country that lacked good stone.

The Count, a great builder of castles in the Netherlands, fell foul of neighbours during a sojourn at the Muiderslot, was seized by them, and murdered in his castle.

The Muiderslot was dismantled and left for a century before taking up life again, in its present form, under the hand of another noble builder, Albrecht of Bavaria.

In the gentler domestic period of the 17th century, writer Hooft, one of the Netherlands most distinguished *littérateurs* and castellan of the Muiderslot for some time, lived and wrote there, gathering round him his 'Muider Circle' of intellectuals such as the physicist Huygens, Van den Burgh and Vondel, the greatest of Dutch poets, besides others.

Doornenburg

Doornenburg's keep, a turreted cube built in the 14th century, is typical of Dutch design and is separated by a running-water moat from its bailey, from which the keep is approached over a wooden bridge that is exposed to fire from both the keep and the bailey buildings. Doornenburg's keep was almost totally destroyed by gunfire during the last war, but has been meticulously restored to its medieval entirety. Today the castle is one of Holland's finest.

Kronborg Castle at Helsingör in Denmark
(Shakespeare's Elsinor) commands the
narrow straight between this part of the
Danish and Swedish coasts.

Denmark

Kronborg

'Hamlet was the doubtfully historic hero of Shakespeare's play of that name,' begins the biographical dictionary's definition of that scion of Denmark's royal house. Not much space is given to the doubting prince in most written descriptions of Kronborg Castle on the Zealand coast at Helsingör (Elsinore) but the historic connection is admitted sufficiently to allow the castle's courtyard and battlements to be used regularly for the enactment of the Bard's play by leading companies from all over the world.

Since the 12th century there had been a fortress here, commanding the western traffic approaches to the straits between Denmark and Sweden when, like the German Barons of the Rhine, the Danish King gathered in his revenue from the merchant vessels, operating a protection racket that would have done credit to Chicago in the 'twenties. This toll was paid by all ships passing the Sound until as recently as 1857.

To back up his system the king needed a strong garrison force. A new castle, Krogen, was built at Helsingör overlooking the sea during the 15th century, a solid quadrilateral pile with ramparts some 3 metres thick. Some of the fabric of this castle was assimilated into the new and much more ornate Kronborg constructed 150 years later, and one may occasionally see an obviously older pointed Gothic window or door arch peeping through the Renaissance work.

Frederick II started building Kronborg in 1574, a time of expansion for Denmark. It took some ten years to complete and shows the influence of contemporary Dutch architecture (Holland being where all the best architects lived) in its general profile.

A century after it was built, Kronborg was captured by the Swedes. Some of the castle garrison attempted to retake it, but failed, in the only warlike action ever seen here. The Swedes, however, shot off the tip of the Great Tower giving it, even today, a flat-hatted look. For all its Renaissance design Kronborg has some serious defence machinery. Its moats are deep and murky and its main walls formidable, with a solid and forbidding look that is rarely seen in the Renaissance period. Its ramparts, famous for their connection with the Shakespeare play, are also serious defenceworks – unlike Denmark's other great castle, Frederiksborg, which was built as an expression of grandeur by Frederick II in the 16th century.

The ramparts at Kronborg. Did Hamlet's father's ghost walk here?

Frederiksborg

Frederiksborg is similarly stamped with the rather heavy Dutch Renaissance style and of all the castle-palaces outside Copenhagen, it is the one with the richest history, and was a favourite residence of many of Denmark's kings.

It is sited (often frozen-in) in the middle of a small lake near the town of Hillerod, where formerly stood a manor house. Apart from the impressive towers, chapel and living quarters, Frederick built two 'summerhouses', one of which was a small pavilion used by the king for intimate sojourns of an unspecified nature. Built in 1580 it contains a bathroom, one of the few recorded in European history. The importance of the installation is illustrated by the name of the pavilion – Badstu, the Bath House.

The king's son Christian IV was born in an age of great buildings. He determined to build a castle more magnificent than any other, tore down much of his father's edifice, and erected the castle we see today on the lake's third islet, a monument based on the style of the châteaux de plaisance of the Loire.

It was partly burned down in 1859. Funds ran out during the re-building and a local brewer offered to help if, he stipulated, the castle were made a national museum. It was agreed, and the Carlsberg Fund completed the restoration.

Ornate Frederiksborg, near Copenhagen, was based on certain châteaux of the Loire, although a more Germanic style is evident here.

Castles of Central Europe

Germany

Heidelberg

Germany's oldest university town lies on the banks of the fast-flowing River Neckar where it begins to spread out into the Rhine plain. The town's tangle of small streets, its low-gabled inns and lodgings and its 'Old Bridge' guarded by two helmeted towers, give it the fairytale air of German stories.

It is Heidelberg's sprawling pink castle, however, that lends the colour of romantic history to the town. Set up on the hill behind the huddled dwellings, this 'flourishing ruin' as it is often called, is an architectural mix in red sandstone, a stone that seems to acquire an almost luminous rosy glow against its green supporting hill in the light of a summer evening.

Started in the 14th century, conquered – and extensively damaged by lightning – in the 16th century, captured again and partly destroyed in the 17th century, and restored during the 19th and 20th centuries, Heidelberg has been the scene of many a master's painting and the venue of many a romantic episode of fact and fiction.

The English painter Turner was captivated by the castle and countryside, and painted landscapes here. In the Royal Gardens (Hortus Palatinus) the German poet Goethe walked and wrote his love-lyrics, inspired it seems, by a succession of willing ladies. In 1814, he fell in love with the lovely Marianne von Willemer, wife of a friend who had 'purchased' her from her mother, a travelling player, when she was a child. Goethe was sixty-five at the time and Marianne just thirty, but the affair was one of the great passions of the poet's life, and could have led to tragedy. In the event, everyone behaved with dignity and Goethe withdrew to write some of his best idylls.

American author Mark Twain and the great French writer and traveller Victor Hugo were charmed by the city and its castle, praising it in print. Composer and pianist Weber, father of German romantic opera, wrote his opera *Der Freischutz* here in the spring of 1820. Robert Schumann was sent here to study law. Heidelberg's influence turned him to music.

The castle on the hill even inspired Sigmund Romberg to produce his energetic musical *The Student Prince*, a light opera that has become part of the modern folklore of the castle and the town.

Today, Heidelberg Castle has been partly restored, with some parts cleverly left in their ruined state. The Krauttürm – the old powder tower – for example, still exposes its interior to the elements, a relic of a French attack in 1689. The Krauttürm contained the town's supply of gunpowder; the French force decided to destroy it, put a match to it and watched in dismay as the 6-metre thick walls merely shuddered and settled back. It took a determined second attack some four years later to produce the scars it now shows to visitors.

The vast cellars of Schloss Heidelberg contain, amongst other alcohol-making equipment, a great vat, large enough to hold nearly a quarter of a million litres and wide enough to support a small dance floor on its top – which it now does. Built in 1751 when the castle's

The richly decorated Renaissance Ottheinrich building in Schloss Heidelberg.

consumption of wine was some
2,000 litres a day, it brought the
cellar's capacity up to nearly
750,000 litres of the white wines of
the region. The giant vat was in fact
used to store the taxes paid annually
in wine by the local growers, later to
be sold to provide revenue. One
may still drink a glass of cool wine in
the dimly-lit vaults of the castle.

The castle itself is a patchwork of
buildings dating from periods
ranging from Gothic to High
Renaissance, and the state of its
interior varies from dank and
draughty to furnished luxury. One
of the finest Renaissance façades in
Europe may be seen in the
Ottheinrich building with its richly
decorated portal and three storeys
of windows. But be careful to check
the nearby sundial – it is almost
three quarters of an hour late.

Above: Heidelberg's pink castle on the
River Neckar; a 'flourishing ruin' that was
started in the 14th century.

Left: Pyrotechnics at Heidelberg castle
illuminate the river.

Right: The main gateway of Burg Eltz,
perched high above a tributary of the
Mosel. Its head-in-the-clouds appearance
lends it an air of fantasy.

The Castle of Cochem on the Mosel has commanded a wide sweep of the vine-clad river for nearly a thousand years.

Burg Eltz

The border regions of Germany display some of the most dramatic examples of Gothic fortress architecture in Europe. The complicated topography gave birth to some of the most dizzying strongholds on crags, spurs, and cliffs and the hazards of being a member of one of dozens of small rival states occupying the region of the Rhine, engendered castle constructions that bristled with look-out towers and defences that were designed to cover attack from any or all directions.

Burg Eltz, just off the main flow of the Mosel west of Koblenz (nearest town Cochem, which has a formidable castle of its own) is considered archetypal. Like several castles of the 12th century, it was divided up into separate dwellings in the residential building area behind its outer defences and shared by several families. Fortified dwellings shared in this way were called *ganerbenburgen*, castles jointly owned, defended and maintained.

Burg Eltz was built up part-by-part like a bird's nest on its rocky promontory, hanging high over the River Eltz and surrounded by dense woods. A glimpse through the forest, across the deep gorge, gives the first hint of the multi-turreted and pinnacled outline, the sheer walls and the completely unscalable defences.

Writer Victor Hugo was prompted to say on his first sight of the castle, 'Through this clearing, like a forest window, the castle appeared. High, enormous, gloomy. I have never seen anything like it.'

The oldest part of the castle is called 'Platt-Eltz' (Flat-Eltz). It was built in late Romanesque style during the 12th century, when the name of the founding family was first heard in the person of Rudolph von Eltz, who witnessed the deed of gift from Emperor Barbarossa. Later the family divided up by marriage into three parts, the Rubenach, Kempenich, and Rodendorf branches, who inherited Burg Eltz as a community of heirs.

Each family built a house of its own behind the great walls adding to them over an extended period from the 15th to the 17th century. Then the families began to move away to take up residence in the nearby towns of Koblenz, Boppard, or Mainz.

Eltz has never been seriously damaged since its construction and its maze of rooms is crowded with domestic and architectural history. Most of the rooms are small – there was little space to expand laterally – and the castle complex is built on several floors, adding to its head-in-the-clouds appearance.

The armoury, generally the first room to be entered, still has a store of weapons and armour, from medieval spears to muzzle-loaders, and displays a 16th century megaphone once used for challenging approaching visitors, and a collection of oriental weaponry, the booty of the Turkish siege of Vienna in the 17th century.

The living room of the Rubenach family has an early form of central heating, a fireplace backplate which when heated would be carried into a nearby bedroom, providing warmth there for the night. Here too, window seats abound, sited to make best use of fading light for sewing or embroidery. The main bedroom of the same family has its large bed raised off the floor a few metres, taking advantage of the fact that warm air rises. A built-in garderobe flushed by rain water channelled from the roof is an example of some inventive domestic plumbing of the early 16th century. This bedroom also has colourful floral and heraldic patterned paintwork over most of its walls and ceiling, said to be the forerunner of wallpaper. Its tiny oratory, a richly decorated chapel, was built out in the form of a bay window so that no earthly life could exist above the heavenly one it represented, in deference to church law.

Other more formal rooms, most designed to a miniature scale as land was at a premium on the rocky crag, are the Elector's Hall – the Eltz family submitted to Baldwin the Elector of Trier in the 14th century and themselves became electors in the following one – garnished with Gobelin tapestries, and a cosy little Knights Hall that has two small interesting plaster-casts on the wall. A clown's mask indicates that anything may be said in the hall by an inmate without offence to another, and above the door a small 'rose of silence' a symbol of discretion, reminds the company that information heard in this room should not be carried outside it.

A large open fireplace is the dominant feature of the kitchen with hooks pendant from the ceiling on which baskets of food would be hung to protect them from the ravages of children and rodents. The German saying 'The food basket must be hung higher' is still used to chastise a greedy child.

Burg Eltz has much to offer the historian and the lay visitor in history and in visual beauty. It is undoubtedly the most breathtaking castle in Germany.

Bürresheim

The noted writer Werner Bornheim had this to say of Bürresheim nestling in the wooded heights of the Eiffel region, 'Here at Schloss Bürresheim a mass of things important and unimportant of everyday life, collected over five centuries, and forming a composite whole, finds its expression. Its magic is among the greatest that historical forces are capable of producing, and as a result, castle and gardens are still really alive. All around the forest sighs, the fountains splash, time stands still.'

The castle's towered profile seems to appear with all the magic of a child's pop-up book-illustration as the traveller rounds a bend in a winding country road near Mayen. Bürresheim is solid enough, with its foundations established back in the 12th century. Bürresheim is, in effect, two castles. On the western end of the elongated plot which is almost entirely encircled by a small river, is the so-called Cologne Castle, first mentioned in 1157 when its owner sold it to the Archbishop of Cologne – and received it back again as a fief, a little power-politics trick of the time to ensure loyalties. It is a cluster of simple and solid towers with narrow defensive archières and massive stonework. The Romanesque castle fell into disuse after extensions were begun on the eastern side some 500 years ago; the once-cherished Knight's Hall was used as a bakery from the 17th century, and other parts were used as a brewery and as cattle stalls.

The eastern side of the castle is the later part of the complex, started

Overleaf: A typical Rhenish fortress-residence, Bürresheim has a domestic appearance which conceals its defence points.

A drawbridge-lifting device. Counterbalancing systems were designed to take much of the hard work out of raising the heavy structure.

in the 15th century and improved and embellished during the two following centuries, with parts of it completed in the ornate Baroque period, giving it a somewhat domestic appearance. However, a cannon passage, designed to increase the mobility of castle weaponry, was built into the massive walls.

Its heavy tower, the upper storey of which is half-timbered in late Gothic style, is the main feature, supported by turrets, conical roofs in glossy slate, and a subordinate round tower capped with a Baroque stepped-and-domed roof. Mullioned windows and dormers give a lighter character to the upper storeys of the castle, imparting a cosy atmosphere to the ensemble that suggests home and hearth.

Bürresheim was lived in continuously from medieval times until the tragic end of the main branch of the family in 1921. The young and attractive Marie Louise, Countess von Renesse had been married just eleven days when her car collided with a horse and cart near the castle. The Countess was killed. Her sister occupied Bürresheim until 1947, when the castle and its treasures of art and furniture became the property of the State. The castle may still be visited; its fabric and contents are a unique monument of Rhenish architectural and domestic history.

Sababurg

Once upon a time, during the period of the Napoleonic Wars, two brothers, Jakob and Wilhelm Grimm, wandered away from their home town of Hanau in Hesse-Kassel into a dark and tangled forest called the Rheinhardswald, where some of the trees are 600 years old. Here the River Weser twists and splashes in its hurry to run quickly through this sombre forest and on to the cold North Sea.

In the Rheinhardswald they found an aged and wizened lady called Dorothy Viehmann who told them many stories of the people of the forest, some of them from old German folklore. The brothers also found a hidden castle called Sababurg, an ancient fortress that had been first built in the 14th century by one of the Archbishops of Mainz. The castle had been used as

an outpost for the people of Mainz to protect them from their Saxon neighbours.

During the numerous disputes in old Germany, Sababurg, then probably called by its medieval name of Zappenborg, was allowed to fall into ruin, but was reconstructed by Count Wilhelm I in 1492, when it became famous for its splendid hunting festivities and the lavish banquets given to visitors from the Court of Kassel, a few leagues to the south. During the Thirty Years War the castle was plundered by Germany's Count Tilly, one of the outstanding soldiers of the century, followed by an occupation by the French. By 1763 Friedrich II had rebuilt the secluded woodland castle into a superb hunting residence, one of the

Left: Sababurg, the secret castle in the Rheinhardswald, a dark forest near Kassel. The Brothers Grimm used this castle for their story of the Sleeping Beauty.

Below: Hohenschwangau in Bavaria, boyhood home of Prince Ludwig, who was to become king at the age of 18.

most magnificent in Europe, whilst retaining the fortress aspect of the earlier castle.

It was at this time the brothers Grimm visited the castle; they used it as the backdrop for the most famous of all their fairytales, *The Sleeping Beauty*.

Hohenschwangau

Ludwig II of Bavaria spent much of his childhood at this castle in the Allgäuer Alps, a Neo-Gothic pile reconstructed by his father Maximilian II on the elevated site of a long-ruined fortress. Of all Ludwig's residences – Herrenchiemsee, Linderhof, Neuschwanstein – Hohenschwangau is the only one that shows any evidence of a building that had been used for family life, although it is said that young Ludwig started his various architectural projects to escape from this home of his youth for his relationship with his mother Queen Marie was not, it appeared, of the most cordial nature.

On the 10th March 1864, Ludwig's father, King of the southern German State, died, and at the age of eighteen, Ludwig had to assume the royal title. His education had not been completed and one of its basic lessons, that of the value of money, had been omitted. A few months later, Ludwig met composer Richard Wagner, who was to be one of the strongest and strangest influences in his short and tragic life. To Wagner, who had become involved in the wrong side of revolution and was now pursued by his creditors, Ludwig's offer of a stipend and a villa must have seemed heaven-sent. Wagner's music and his heroic characters of Lohengrin, Tannhauser and others, so affected the narcissistic Ludwig that he took refuge in them from his royal duties, often cloaking himself in the part of Lohengrin.

Wagner himself also came under the young king's spell. 'I fly to him as a lover', he wrote once to a friend. 'He is like a god. If I am Wotan, then he is my Siegfried.' To add to the court's suspicions of what then would have been a disastrously unnatural relationship, Wagner made other gushing statements. The friendship is even now a subject for historians to wrangle over,

although much of what was written was, it should be remembered, in the florid idiom and the narrow moral confines of the day.

Ludwig's three romantic castles in Bavaria sprang largely from his association with Wagner. That, and the fact that this royal dreamer shunned the glare of public life, building his own cocoon of fantasy – even living mainly by artificial light with which his castles were amply supplied.

Hohenschwangau, which a contemporary called 'the little gingerbread castle on the Alpsee', was the home of his childhood, a fact which was undoubtedly the third of the compelling influences that shaped his life and his building projects.

Hohenschwangau, restored by Ludwig's father, had been lavishly decorated in Biedermeier style, and on his accession Ludwig suggested, quite reasonably, that he have his own apartments fitted out there. The reply that he could not possibly disturb the servants that already lived there provoked him into over-compensation when he finally had his way. He refurbished the castle far more extravagantly than he at first intended.

Today, Hohenschwangau is part of the double attraction of the region. More historically significant than its close neighbour Neuschwanstein, it is over-shadowed both topographically and architecturally by the latter, although its interior is a magnificent example of romantic revivalism.

Neuschwanstein

A dream castle built by a dream king is often the description given to the castle of Neuschwanstein, towering half-way to heaven on a wooded spur overlooking the Pollat Gorge in the Bavarian Alps.

Germany's most visited castle is shrouded by dark pines and steep slopes and frequently cloaked in grey mountain mist, yet pilgrims toil year-round to its barbican entrance high in the Alpine foothills behind the small village of Hohenschwangau.

Neuschwanstein saw no great sieges, was part of no battles, has indeed no past to speak of, since it was completed less than hundred years ago. When young Ludwig II, King of Bavaria took possession in

1886 of the newly finished
Neuschwanstein for the brief
remainder of his life (he lived there
only 102 days before his death by
drowning after he had been
declared insane), the first motor
transport was beginning to putter
along the roads of Germany, and
Germany's Iron Chancellor,
Bismarck was already an old man.

However, 'Mad' Ludwig's fairy
castle, without doubt the most
romantic edifice of the so-called
Romantic era, has brought untold
pleasure to the unending groups of
tourists (nearly a million every
year) who visit this 19th century
white-and-green extravaganza.

This fantastic showplace grew, in
essence, from the brush of Christian
Jank, a theatre painter whose
watercolour sketches inspired much
of the Wagnerian mood of this vast
complex, although the court
architect, Edward Riedel, provided
the final construction expertise, and
no doubt modified the higher flights
of Jank's artistic fancy.

King Ludwig had been an
enigma all his life. This shy,
hypersensitive youth, tremendously
handsome in an aesthetic way, was
a great horseman, swimmer and
athlete. His weird night rides
through the Bavarian countryside,
and his later nocturnal journeys in a
golden sleigh drawn by six
dapple-grey horses and attendants
in 18th century garb, must have
been a daunting sight for his simple
peasants.

Above: The singers' or minstrels' hall at
Neuschwanstein was modelled on
Wartburg Castle in Thuringia. It was never
used during Ludwig's life.

Left: 'A dream castle built by a dream king,'
said a German writer of the fantastic
Schloss Neuschwanstein, built by
Bavaria's king Ludwig in the late 19th
century.

Although most of the interior of Neuschwanstein is solidly Gothic, Romanesque or Byzantine, Ludwig, strongly identifying in fantasy with both Lohengrin and Tannhauser, built on the castle's third floor an artificial stalactite 'Grotto of Venus' in the Tannhauser mood, and the castle's Great Hall, whose décor, with its swan theme, evokes the legend of Lohengrin.

The Minstrels' Hall, the original of which, at Wartburg Castle near Eisenach in Thuringia, was the first stimulus to Ludwig's desire to build Schloss Neuschwanstein, is a magnificent room, perhaps more important than the throne room itself. All have such lavish treatment which, coupled with the height of the castle's location and its godlike views, lend an air of total unreality, a condition which one feels Ludwig himself must have known for much of his strange life.

This castle-in-the-sky, though short its history and confused its architecture, is one of the great attractions of Bavaria to historians and tourists alike. And no literature of the region or the period is complete without a survey of the dramatic Schloss Neuschwanstein.

The Rhine

The best known part of the Rhine is almost certainly the section between Koblenz and Bingen, the rocky steep-sided valley that has a castle on almost every bend of the vine-clad river, and includes the famous Loreley Rock. Certainly more river-cruisers seem to traverse this part of the Rhine, extolling its beauties and its history to its holiday cargo of passengers than any other stretch of the river. And with some reason, for this part of the ancient waterway is undoubtedly the most beautiful.

The Rhine, trade route and link between western European nations rises from the Swiss heights near Italy to the North like an aquatic autobahn, along which for centuries all commercial traffic passed, and from castles on the bank of which many German knights, electors, petty kings and the like extracted tolls from passing merchant vessels. The river scene has changed little in five centuries. Some of the castles have been given a stone-and-mortar facelift in the cause of tourism

perhaps, but they still command their part of the river, they still grow their vines as they did in the Middle Ages, and they still collect their tolls, albeit in entrance fees.

Drachenfels
Drachenfels Castle, less than ten kilometres south of the Federal German capital, Bonn, sits high on the east bank of the Rhine on one of the Siebengebirge – the Seven Mountains – from which the stones of its own fabric were quarried, as

were those of the great Cologne Cathedral nearby. So much stone was taken from the small group of hills that an Act was passed in the 17th century to prevent them disappearing completely! Even so, much of the castle collapsed under earlier unrestricted mining leaving little more than its keep. Built in the 12th century by the local Archbishops, Drachenfels (Dragon's Rock) was home to one of Germany's Crusader knights, his family adopting a silver dragon as

Marksburg above Braubach on the Rhine. This castle is one of the few that has survived the turbulent regional warfare almost intact.

Marksburg which stands above Braubach. The gunloops of its great bailey shows the iron snouts of the castle's battery, and one feels that the piles of cannonballs on display there could still be lobbed across the river to crash down on some defiant Florentine merchant. This stronghold is one of the few that has not been inherited as a ruin and subjected to romantic restoration but, with some additions in the 17th and 18th centuries, has reached the 20th century in almost the same state as it was in the 15th century.

One of the oldest castles, the Marksburg was mentioned in A.D. 882. It belonged to the Counts of Katzenelnbogen in the 13th century. This large and belligerent Rhenish family owned (or captured) several castles on the river and like many other robber knights of Germany during the Interregnum (the rulerless period preceding the election of Rudolf of Habsburg in 1273) divided their time between fighting their neighbours and raising tolls at gunpoint from the unfortunates who passed within range of their weapons.

Until the 17th century Braubach and its castle lived in the path of countless catastrophes. Uncaring mercenaries put their savage mark upon the town, plague struck town and castle during the Thirty Years War, flood carried away much of Braubach, and the Marksburg was used as a last refuge for the peasants against an onslaught by the Swedes. Later the castle was strengthened against attack by firearms – a report of 1588 lists six cannon, all covering the Rhine approaches.

The Marksburg played its most recent part in the history of the Rhine when in March 1945 allied guns demolished the top of its central tower. Its own did not reply.

its armorial device.

In legend Siegfried killed a dragon living here in one of the mountain caves and bathed in its blood. Today the fable lends its narrative to the name of a wine, Drachen Blut (Dragon's Blood), harvested from the vines that grow here on the sunny slopes of the Siebengebirge.

Marksburg

Perhaps the most grim and businesslike castle on the river is the

Boppard

About ten kilometres upriver in a generally southerly direction lies Boppard, where, in the 14th century, the Elector Baldwin of Trier built one of the strongest fortifications on the Rhine. Despite a fire some 500 years ago, the keep still displays some historic frescoes painted at the time the castle was built. A few kilometres upstream are the two rival castles of Katz and Maus.

Katz

Katz, its full name Neu-Katzenelnbogen, rises high over the Rhineside town of Saint Goarshausen, dwarfing the colourful string of old houses that lines the river's edge. It was built around the late 14th century in the last days of the robber knights – to protect the immediate region and to levy tolls from passing river traffic by the family from whom the castle took its name. Like many Rhine castles, its revenue was coveted by all who had the slightest excuse to lay claim to the local territory and Katz passed violently through several hands. In common with several neighbouring toll stations, it was destroyed by the ravaging French in the early 1800s. It is now a natural science college.

Maus

Close neighbour on the same bank of the Rhine is Maus Castle, so

Katz towers above St. Goarshausen and the Rhine. Built in the 14th century to levy tolls from passing river traffic, it is now a college.

named in cheeky defiance of the ruling Katzenelnbogen clan. 'Where there is a cat there also must be a mouse', scoffed the Katzenelnbogen family, whose clear intention it was to gobble up the next-door stronghold in due course. But Kuno von Falkenstein, Archbishop of Trier, built solidly.

Maus is recognized as one of the best-planned defensive works in the Rhine region. Its squarish layout with small corner turrets surrounding a round keep indicates advanced military thinking in the 14th century fortress design.

Rheinfels

Opposite Katz on the high west bank of the Rhine above Saint Goar sprawls Rheinfels, ruined now, its sightless windows framing the sky and its battlements decorated with wild vines. Built in 1245 by the ubiquitous Katzenelnbogen, it was the largest burg on the Rhine – and was yet another toll station. Its first test came soon after it was completed, when it successfully stood siege for a year against the League of Rhenish towns. When the

Right: Burg Maus, built in defiance of the larger Katz, sits just a whisker away from its neighbour, with no more than a nibbled tower-top to show the passage of time.

Below: On the west bank of the Rhine near St. Goar sprawls 13th century Rheinfels, once the largest castle on the Rhine.

Counts of Katzenelnbogen later built Katz, directly opposite, the family significantly increased its control of the entire Rhine Valley and its trade.

Rheinfels succumbed to French revolutionary troops who captured it during the summer campaign of 1794, when the French under General Moreau cleared the Mosel and the Rhine of Prussian resistance and laid siege to Mainz. Two years later, Rheinfels was demolished.

Schönburg

South of Rheinfels, is Oberwesel, a small town which boasts its own aerie in the heights above the nestling town, Schönburg Castle. This 12th to 16th century fortress is shielded from landward attacks by a vast and solid wall known as the 'Hohemantel' (high mantle) a defence system that often took the place of a bergfried. A century after it was built Schönburg was extended by the two families then living in it, who strengthened it

against the envious appetites of the Lords of Trier, the malevolent plans of the Reich and of the Palatinate Counts of the Rhine. It was bought by a German-American in the 1880s and today is an international youth hostel.

Pfalz

The Pfalz or Pfalzgrafenstein, as it was once called, is perhaps the most bizarre castle on the Rhine – or more correctly in this case, *in the* Rhine, near Kaub.

The small fortress was built on a long sliver of rock and shale in the middle of the fast flowing river, like 'a ship of stone eternally floating on the Rhine, eternally at anchor', as the ubiquitous Victor Hugo put it. Hugo's description of this castle was apt. It does look as though it was deliberately fashioned like a ship, its upstream prow for ever dividing the waters of the Rhine and its bulwarks high above the racing

Schönburg, once a vital part of river defence, now a youth hostel.

Left: The 'Hohemantel' or high wall was the main shield of Schönburg, taking the place of a keep or bergfried.

Below: 'Like a ship of stone floating on the Rhine' said writer Victor Hugo of Pfalz. Here a modern cruise ship passes the island castle.

flow. The observation turrets and the tower roof which give Pfalz the look of a toy galleon date from the 17th century. Built by an earlier Ludwig of Bavaria as a toll station, Pfalz had a decided advantage over some of the hilltop fortresses that also played the same predatory game for it was at water-level in a position that could detect the passing of anything larger than a minnow.

Left: Gutenfels castle overlooks its small neighbour Pfalz down at water level. Built by the Falkenstein family in the early 13th century, it is now a hotel.

Below: An historic marriage took place at Stahleck Castle in 1194. It ended the feud between two leading medieval families.

Gutenfels

Overlooking mid-river Pfalz is Gutenfels Castle built a century earlier by the Falkenstein family, members of which later supplied Trier with its archbishops. Not a generation after it was completed, it fell into the hands of the Palatine Elector, who later owned both this Romanesque castle and its smaller partner Pfalz.

Stahleck

Stahleck Castle above Bacharach is today a youth hostel, ringing to the laughter of children after a long and grim history that earned it notoriety as early as 1136. An historically important marriage took place there

The courtyard of Stahleck. Like several Rhine castles it is now used by the German Youth Hostel Association.

in 1194 between Agnes von Stahleck and Welfe Heinrich, her childhood sweetheart and son of Henry the Lion, head of the Guelphs, an espousal that ended the long feud between the families of Guelphs and Hohenstaufen which had been a major cause of European conflict at this time. When Agnes and her childless son died, the

Hohenstaufen Emperor Frederick II gave the castle to Ludwig of Bavaria, who then owned two of the main tax-levying stations of the Rhine, Pfalz and Stahleck. The castle was besieged by the Swedes and the Spaniards during the Thirty Years War, and was partly destroyed by the troops of Louis XIV in 1689. Painstaking

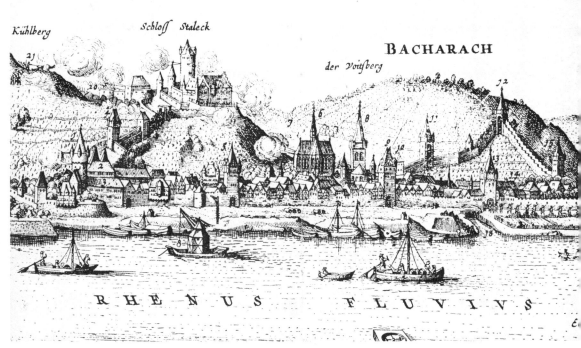

Stahleck Castle and Bacharach, with Rhine traffic; an engraving made in the 17th century.

Austria

Hohensalzburg

Salzburg, city of music and bridges and baroque spires on the River Salzach has a squat, brooding castle nestling in the wooded hills above, overlooking its every move – Hohensalzburg, 11th century castle of the bishop-princes of Austria for six hundred years.

The good burghers of the town first saw the interior of the castle when a 15th century bishop invited them to dinner at Hohensalzburg. They had just been granted full city rights by their emperor Frederick III. However, a bitter struggle between Pope and Emperor for supremacy in Christendom was being waged, and instead of the promised banquet they were seized, bound and threatened with immediate death unless they agreed to submit to government by the church. They agreed. The city then gradually developed in its appearance from dour teutonic to graceful Renaissance – the Salzburg we see today.

In vain did the peasants, who had not welcomed the proposed change, later besiege Hohensalzburg. The castle had been built to last, despite some fanciful additions in the 15th century. Later additions to the castle have leavened its grim outward aspect a little, but the interiors give much more information about life in the 16th and 17th centuries than the heavy exterior elevations.

restoration since 1900 has brought Stahleck, one of the most visually dramatic castles of the Rhine, back to its former glory.

During almost the entire length of a river journey from Bonn upstream to Bingen, one is in sight of a Rhine castle, towering on a rocky crag, dominating a fold of the river, or nestling into the vineyard slopes.

Overleaf: Hohensalzburg, above Salzburg. Says Austrian history: 'Bishop Dietrich envisaged the city, Lodon carved the vision in stone, and Mozart set it to music.'

Festung (fortress) Kufstein stands on a wooded hill at a bend in the Inn Valley, a heavy stronghold brooding over the town since the 12th century.

the 15th century. Thereafter it lay in its eagle's nest, unmolested for generations, until in 1504 German Emperor Maximilian, on his campaign to rid the region of Hungarians, brought up a couple of great cannon and shot Kufstein full of holes. This caused a local sensation for the castle had been considered impregnable. Obligingly, Maximilian repaired the castle and built several more towers including the strongest of the castle, the Kaisertürm.

The castle was being used as an arsenal during the Spanish wars of the 18th century when Archduke Max Emanuel's troops attacked. Because of its strength much of Kufstein survived and the fortress is now a national museum.

Switzerland

Chillon

The Château de Chillon, Switzerland's most distinguished castle, is tucked up close against the eastern shore of Lake Geneva (Lac Leman to the French-speaking locals), a drawbridge away from solid land.

The Swiss National Railway runs along the edge of the shore past the old wooden entrance bridge and the main Montreux-Lausanne road sweeps along a few metres up the steep lakeside banks. Higher still, one of Europe's great motorways snakes through the fir-clad hills. But none of these 20th century transport systems distracts from the peace and solitude of the water-lapped château.

Benevolently colourful in morning light, Chillon, parts of which are a thousand years old, assumes a heavier, more bellicose character as the sun travels west, black shadows growing slowly into the darkening waters below its sheer walls. By late afternoon the castle takes on the look of the Chillon of the 13th century, a fortress on the landward side, and a princely palace facing the lake.

Also facing the farther shore and the French Savoy are the high narrow windows of the castle's prison, a dank and gloomy hall with the rough uncut rock on which Chillon was built still visible. Here the château's main historical figure, Bonivard, Prior of Saint Victor at Geneva, was chained to the fifth

Kufstein

One of the eastern gates to Austria, the fortress at Kufstein hovers above a bend in the crooked Inn Valley, where the river twists round into Germany's Bavaria before re-entering Austria to flow into the Danube.

Built at various times between the 12th and 13th centuries, it illustrates clearly in its heavyweight architecture, the wild conditions in the Tyrol during that period. Its enormously thick-walled round tower – more a ponderous roundhouse than a lofty citadel – was its prime defence, a sure bastion against the all-too-regular tides of misfortune that flowed past the region.

Ludwig 'The Bearded' strengthened this elevated fort in

pillar from the entrance – a monument of despair still to be seen with its grisly chain and cuffs. Bonivard had unwisely favoured the Reformation, which he had attempted to introduce to Geneva, and for six dreary years this martyr sat chained, until freed by the Bernese in 1536.

The good father was later immortalized by Lord Byron, who visited the castle with Shelley in 1816. Byron, moved by the pathos of the priest's suffering, was prompted to write his poem *The Prisoner of Chillon* in homage to Bonivard. A couple of generations earlier Rousseau had lodged in this grim pile and had located a scene of his *La Nouvelle Heloise* there. Byron, who admired the works of Rousseau, wrote to a friend, 'I have travelled all Rousseau's ground – with the Heloise before me, and am struck to a degree with the force and accuracy of his descriptions – the beauty of their reality...'

Visitors during the Romantic period of the 19th century were many. Dumas followed Byron and Hans Christian Andersen stayed there a year or two later. In 1846 Charles Dickens, doyen of English writers of the period, visited the castle.

Said Dumas, 'The martyr's prison has become a temple, its pillar an altar. Each noble heart and each lover of liberty comes a long way to pray where he suffered... You bend over the worn flagstones to look for a trace of his footprints...' as indeed does any visitor to Chillon today.

French novelist Gustave Flaubert was similarly impressed by the example of medieval suffering. He wrote, 'we reach the prisoner's

Bonivard's 13th century prison at the Château de Chillon. He was chained to one of the pillars for several years, finally being released on 29th March 1536.

Above: Switzerland's most famous castle, Chillon, lies a moat's width away from the shore of Lake Geneva.

Left: The Knight's Hall at Chillon, with 16th and 17th century paintings of Bernoise armorial bearings on the far wall.

Right: Aigle, one of the Savoyard advance strongholds in the Valais region of Switzerland.

room. There is a ring one foot from the ground and all around it the stone is worn from his steps doing the same semi-circle . . . Byron's name is written on the third column . . . then I went to the prisoner's column, Victor Hugo's name was written with a pencil and George Sand's engraved with a knife . . .'

Byron's name is still there today.

Although this lakeside château had been an active defence post since Roman days it is noted more for its association with the Romantic Period than with its harsh medieval history. Its situation, on the truly beautiful lake at the foot of the Alps with the great mountain range of the Dents Du Midi as a backdrop for its machicolations and pointed pantiled roofs, is superb, and its colourful series of wall and ceiling paintings dating from the 13th century ensure it a place in the history of art as the writing of Byron and others secure it a niche in literature.

Aigle

Not far from the eastern end of Lake Geneva lies the château of Aigle, dozing in its vineyards. It lies in the broad Rhone Valley, perhaps one of the most beautiful late medieval fortresses in Europe – just outside the residential area, on gentle slopes and surrounded by the vines that later in the season will produce the grapes for Vin d' Aigle and Yvorne, the two wines of the region. This part of the country, and the vineclad north shores of the lake itself supply most of the wines of Switzerland, relatively unknown outside the country, and Aigle is now a wine museum and vintners conference centre.

The castle was by 1240 a stronghold of the Prince of Savoy, used as an outpost of that Duchy against the captured lands of the Vaud region. It was almost completely destroyed some 200 years later by the Savoyards' natural enemies, the Princes of Berne – who immediately rebuilt it into the castle seen today.

The Swiss Confederation had formed in 1291, and with many other mountain and lake strongholds in the region, Aigle had been captured in the name of liberty, which at the time meant freedom from the yoke of the Habsburgs. Basle, Berne, Fribourg, Zurich and other regions had become city states, and the castle at Aigle became a bailiff's château. After the French Revolution, at a time when little interest was taken in the castles or palaces of Europe, Aigle was used as the district prison and this state continued until 1972.

Simple in plan, with a roughly rectangular layout, curtain walls cornered by three drum towers and a fourth bergfried-like square tower in the north-west corner, Aigle's castle has a guardroom built over its main gate allowing formidable machicolations over the arched entrance. The covered elevated walkway or allure round the outer walls still dominates the approaches to the castle.

Left: The circular layout of the roof trusses and beams of the old Corner Tower at Aigle which the Savoyards used as a keep during the 15th century.

Right: The Great Tower of Aigle in the north-west corner of the castle, built by the Bernese.

Liechtenstein

Vaduz

Vaduz, capital city of Liechtenstein, last of the Teutonic Principalities, lies in the valley of the young Rhine, the frontier between this little country and the Swiss canton of Saint Gallen for about 30 kilometres.

Vaduz has seen its share of the turbulence of passing history. Lying at the crossroads of Alpine traffic, a much-travelled route since pre-Roman days, the little principality has seen wars, revolts and famines, rulers both benign and harsh, plunder and murder by foreign troops passing through on their way to greater conquests.

The castle, still home of the Princely House, rests on a powerful corner of a rock formation

Above: The fortress of Vaduz, capital of Liechtenstein, last of the independent Teutonic states.

Top left: The coat-of-arms of the ruling Prince Franz Joseph II and State of Liechtenstein.

Left: A stronghold since prehistoric times, Gutenberg Castle at Balzers in Liechtenstein is a private home.

overlooking Vaduz itself. It dates from the 13th century, was totally destroyed in 1499 by the neighbouring Swiss and rebuilt soon afterwards, wisely with two new immensely strong and broad round tower-bastions and a west wall. Three gates hamper impetuous entry, and the bergfried in the east part of the castle could still make a stubborn blockhouse today.

Gutenberg

A few kilometres south of Vaduz the Rhine valley plain is broken by a single rocky upthrust of land, rising some 60 metres above the plain. A natural defence position, it was soon utilised by strategists of the 12th century, both to subdue the immediate region and as a protection for the town of Balzers at its foot.

First a wall was thrown up around the crag. To this further circular walls were added as a second line of protection, then garrison living-quarters were built, and finally domestic buildings were raised.

Fairly recently, artefacts dating back to 3000 B.C. were found on the site's southern slope.

Gutenberg Castle still stands on its isolated crag, secure, intact and used now as a private home.

Czechoslovakia

Karlstejn

There are no less than 40,000 buildings of historic interest registered in Czechoslovakia, many of them castles of various periods, including a large number of medieval structures. The astonishing figure of 4,000 is given as the total number of surviving castles in this country, a region of Europe that began its history earlier than most.

The formidable Karlstejn was built by Charles IV, the 'Priest's Emperor' in 1348, in the forests above the River Berounka, a stronghold for the secure keeping of the crown jewels and sacred relics, including a reputed piece of the True Cross. These were placed in the castle's chapel and its walls lined with precious stones, gems which may still be seen glittering faintly in the medieval gloom of the small chapel at Karlstejn.

Charles, having accomplished the building of his shrines, retired to the castle for a life of religious contemplation and forbade visitors. His wife, however, was not as submissive as his vassals. She gained entry to the castle dressed as a pageboy, with results that history does not record. However, her nocturnal visit gave birth to the Czech comedy *A Night at Karlstejn* a show that is still performed in the cour d'honneur of the castle today.

Pernstejn

Standing alone in the forest of the Czecho-Moravian highlands is a tall and rugged castle of the Middle Ages – once the property of the Lords of Pernstejn.

The Hussite Wars – internal Bohemian struggles led by peasant's son John Huss, theologian and friend of Bohemia's King Wenceslaus, paved the way for the country's freedom from the rule of the church, destroying many a

Karlstejn, in the forests above Czechoslovakia's Berounka River, was built to house holy relics in the 14th century.

Bohemian castle, Pernstejn included. Many of its treasures, valuables that had been confiscated by the Church, survived and were returned to their rightful owners, the nobility. The castle was rebuilt in 1457 by the two brothers Pernstejn and refurbished in the 16th century. It has one of the finest examples of a true barbican, built to protect the main entry of the castle, which was in fact a small door high above ground level. A completely separate fort, the barbican is joined to the main building by an elevated enclosed bridge, a narrow corridor that made any forced entry to the castle itself virtually impossible.

Castles of the Mediterranean and the Levant

Spain

The Iberian peninsular, lying between the Christian world and that of Islam was a natural bridge over which the early Moslem armies obtained a foothold in Europe. Visigothic Spain had only a few years previously seen the last of the Roman legions depart, and by A.D. 711 the first of the Moslem hordes had arrived under Tarik El Ziyad from across the narrow strait that separated Spain from North Africa. The invaders landed at a rocky promontory they named Gabel el Tarik (Gibraltar) after their leader.

The country's natives, or its occupiers, threw up defences against opposing forces from every direction, within and outside the country itself. The military works thus created illustrate the different cultures that held sway in Spain for several centuries and show the successive waves of castle-building that followed each upheaval.

Most were built for starkly military purposes, and were harsh uncompromising forts, sited on hilltops bare of surrounding greenery. Some others, later castles built during the reconquest of the 15th and 16th centuries, were as much palaces as fortresses and showed it in their fanciful design: their battlements owed as much to architectural whim as to defence, their gunloops afforded a view for the resident ladies, and their walls were of a quality that could often be demolished by a pitchfork.

Nevertheless, Spain is rich in surviving castles, the greatest concentration being in the province of Segovia.

The Alcazar of Segovia
This is the most venerated castle in Spain. The Alcazar (fortress) was already a national monument in the time of Alfonso the Wise, the 13th century king of Leon and Castile noted for building, his code of laws and knowledge of astronomy. It was in the Alcazar that he studied the cosmos and advanced the theory that the earth moved around the sun. The fact that the castle was struck by an enormous bolt of lightning shortly afterwards was taken as a Divine comment on his theories. In 1383 another king, John I, authorized the Christian calendar to begin with the birth of Christ. Christopher Columbus came here to beg Queen Isabella for funds that resulted in his discovery of America. The tyrannic Philip II of Spain married his niece, Anne of Austria,

The Alcazar of Segovia was partly destroyed by fire in 1862, but was magnificently restored. This is the Ambassador's Salon, in heavily stylized Moorish décor.

Above: The great Coca, castle-palace of bishops, scene of lavish feasts and bacchanalian nights during its heyday in the 15th century.

Left: The Alcazar of Segovia in Spain, a royal castle transformed into a royal palace during the 15th century.

at the Alcazar of Segovia after his first wife Mary Tudor of England had died, after his bid to gain the hand of Elizabeth I had failed, and after his second wife Isabella of France had also perished. Philip restored the castle, unfortunately replacing most of the sophisticated Moorish structure with a more severe style, which included turrets and pointed roofs.

The Alcazar was used to house a college of artillery during the last century until it was razed by fire, destroying most of Philip's work. The 19th century restorations have left this castle with a slightly Teutonic appearance, although the John II tower built in the 15th century remains almost untouched.

Coca

The massive palace-fort of Coca in the umbrella forests north of Segovia was the scene of a lavish and unbridled fiesta. Its 15th century owner, the Bishop of Seville, had invited a vast number of guests to a banquet. Music and revelling was riotous, until the bishop requested silence. To mark the occasion, he said, he intended to present every lady with a gold ring set with precious stones, and proceeded to hand out one to every female in sight. He parted with several hundred rings that evening.

Similar excesses are illustrated in the design of the massive castle itself. Coca, the immense, the fantastic, was part of a four-castle 'square', designed as a strategic defence point during civil strife in Castile. It was built by Moslem Mudéjar workers who were then considerably more cultured, architecturally, than Christian designers and artisans, and the vast façades of Coca are fine examples of Arab influence on Gothic structure, a mix that resulted in a uniquely Spanish style. Most of the Spanish castles of the time were built for genuine military purposes but Coca, built in rose-coloured brick, showing massively thick walls to the outside world, with thousands of crenellations fronting its wall-walks, and with towers and bartizan turrets by the dozen, is really a dressed-up palace, a dandy trying to look like a soldier. It gives its secret away in its outer decorations, its fluted and filigreed brickwork, and by its inner walls, the reverse sides of which are rubble faced by brick to give an appearance of solid strength.

No battles were fought over Coca, no guns fired in anger from its loops, but this giant edifice is, never-theless, one of the wonders of Spain.

San Servando
Toledo lies in almost the centre of the land-mass of modern Spain, just south of Madrid. The Romans had built a fort here on the north bank of the Tagus, the long river that meets the sea beyond Lisbon in Portugal, and the Moors had also built a castle here to guard their city. When Toledo was re-conquered in 1085, the first important Moslem city to be recaptured by Christian forces after nearly four centuries of Moorish occupation, the castle of San Servando was used as a Benedictine monastery.

Ruy Diaz de Vivar, known as El Cid, Spain's great hero of the 11th century who was engaged in restoring the Iberian peninsular to the Christians, visited San Servando. The castle-monastery features in the lengthy poem about El Cid and his exploits. The epic records an attack by Arab fanatics on San Servando and its subsequent burning, and also notes that El Cid lived there for his last years after banishment by a monarch envious of his successes.

Later, after its religious community had departed, King Alfonso gave San Servando to the Knights Templar. It was patiently rebuilt in the late 11th century, fortified, and a keep added. Little is known about this stage of San Servando as it was abandoned when the Templar's Order was disbanded.

The present castle was the work of another prelate of Spain in the 15th century, an age when the church's military might was often superior to that of the monarch, and the church's wish was often law. Its design was also influenced by its Moslem Mudéjar builders (many of whom stayed on to work in Spain after the Reconquest) and its Gothic structure lightened by Arab detail.

Above: Built in 1240 by Frederick II of the Hohenstaufens, Castello del Monte is a mixture of Gothic and classical architecture, unique in Europe.

Left: Coca's outer defences looked impressive, with its gunloops and its battered (outward sloping) walls. It was, however, more palace than fortress.

Italy

Castello del Monte

One of the most significantly intellectual of early medieval kings, Frederick II of the Hohenstaufen line, built, in his middle life, a hunting lodge in Southern Italy. At least, he called it a hunting lodge, but its plan gave birth to a more solid construction than that.

Castello del Monte, built 1240 on a steep mountain in Apulia, is still starkly silhouetted against the skyline, an immensely solid piece of masonry, the plans of which were reputedly drawn up by the Emperor himself. It is octagonal in concept and shape, and repeats the form throughout. Its eight short walls are flanked by eight octagonal corner towers and the central courtyard is also eight-sided, the rooms being arranged regularly around the octagonal theme. A child's plan perhaps, regular, symmetrical and simple, but resulting in a majestic example of the secular building of its time. Some historians aver that it was not designed as a stronghold and some of its delicate building

material and sculpture would seem to confirm this, but its purpose was obviously twofold, as much a secure resting place as a mews for Frederick's hunting birds.

The styles of Del Monte are mixed; the Hohenstaufen monarch often favoured Byzantine and Moslem architecture, but here one has classic Corinthian columns and a pediment at the gateway, and Gothic windows set into stout walls that are certainly Gothic in character.

Castello Nuovo

Charles of Anjou, son of Louis VIII of France had allowed himself to be made an instrument of the papacy in order to secure for himself the former Hohenstaufen Empire. When Frederick II died, Charles imprisoned the rest of the Hohenstaufen family in the lonely stone lodge. He strengthened other castles in Italy for his own use, and began work in 1283 on an extensive fortification at Naples, Castello Nuovo, New Castle, one of the most powerful forts in the country.

Castello Nuovo was started in the

Castello Nuovo, Naples, has a history that dates from the 13th century, although its present appearance stems from the 15th.

same year as Caernarvon and Harlech in Wales, two of the greatest castles of England's Edward I and for approximately the same reason, that of subduing the populace. Castello Nuovo was embellished and enlarged over the years that followed, more to improve its appearance than its defences.

Castel Sant' Angelo
Dominated by its drum-like shell keep that was built in A.D. 135 as the mausoleum of the Emperor Hadrian, the Castel Sant' Angelo on the banks of the Tiber was converted into a stronghold for the papacy by Leo IV when the Saracens were about to engulf Rome in the 6th century A.D.

Sant' Angelo was besieged

several times with, on at least one occasion, a pope (Gregory VII) lodged inside with his retinue, and (in the 11th century) Henry IV of Germany on the outside.

The squat, compact castle was up-dated in 1492 to meet the firearms threat that had even then radically changed siege warfare, when the current Pope ordered bastions to be added to the round towers at the corners of the castle. The towers and the rotund shell keep were lowered to serve as gun-platforms at the same time, while the interior of the keep was finely decorated as papal living quarters.

Right: On the river Tiber not far from the Vatican stands the Castel Sant' Angelo, once the tomb of Emperor Hadrian.

Far right: Kolossi Castle near Limassol in Cyprus. It was given with its estate to the Knights of St. John Crusaders in 1210.

The interior of the 12th century chapel of Krak des Chevaliers, the castle of the Knights of St. John.

Cyprus

Kolossi

The origins of the castle at Kolossi some 10 kilometres west of Limassol in Southern Cyprus are unknown, but the site may have previously been held by a small Byzantine force. It was certainly in existence when the estate itself was given to the Knights of St. John of Jerusalem (the Hospitallers) in 1210 in the name of their cause.

When the Crusaders were forced to withdraw to Limassol after the fall of Acre, they decided to develop Kolossi Castle as one of the main centres of their Order in the East, although, in fact, events overtook them and the Order headquarters were moved to Rhodes. Kolossi suffered several raids by the fierce Mameluke armies from Egypt during the following years, probably due more to the fact that it was a fertile vine-growing region than to the presence of the remaining Hospitaller possessions. The square-keep of Kolossi has had a rough journey through history, being subjected to regular attacks by various Mediterranean factions through its 800 years, to survive to the 20th century with remarkably little damage to its massive donjon, although most of its outbuildings have disappeared.

Syria

Krak des Chevaliers

A profusion of castles punctuated the lands of the Levant, from the shores of Turkey and the Taurus Mountains almost to the borders of Egypt in the south – the works of Arabs, Crusaders, Armenians, Turks. All now stand silent, deserted in arid and desolate regions visited rarely by historian or tourist.

The greatest of the Crusader Castles is undoubtedly the sprawling Krak des Chevaliers, fortress of the Knights of St. John, and still in a state of remarkable preservation. The oldest part of the Krak was erected during the first half of the 12th century and finished in the 13th, and bears considerable similarity of layout to the Edwardian castles in North Wales constructed a century or so later. By the time this castle, one of a number built in a similar style and

complexity, was completed, the
Crusaders had learned a great deal
from their Islamic foes and had
incorporated much that was new in
defence techniques into their
designs.

The number and quality of the
Crusaders' castles put down in the
rocky soil of the region is
astonishing. For two hundred years
Christian architects feverishly
constructed castles and living
quarters for their armies of
dedicated knights, building castle
after castle on inhospitable
promontories down the length of the
coast. The sheer size of some defies
belief – some 170,000 tons of stone
were moved to strengthen Saone,
one of the castles in the North. The
cellars of another, Château Margat,
were built to hold provisions for a
thousand men for five years of
siege.

The Krak des Chevaliers in
northern Syria was one of a chain of
five posts guarding a strategic gap in
the defence of the region.

It was a vast project, a stronghold
that became the foremost bastion of
Christianity in the East, a rallying
point for many campaigns into the
interior. 'It sticks like a bone in the
throat of Islam' said a Moslem
scribe. They besieged it at least
twelve times without success, such
was its strength.

It fell eventually, not through any
flaw in its design, but by trickery.
An army of Mohammed gathered at
the gates, laid siege to the small
garrison of combatant
knight-monks. On 5th March 1271,
they withdrew to an inner ring of
defences from where they could not
be dislodged. The besiegers, finding
force useless, resorted to guile. A
letter was presented to the castle's
force purporting to be from the
Grand Commander of the Order at
Tripoli, instructing the knightly
garrison to surrender. They did so,
later to be informed that the letter
was a forgery. Thus on 8th April the
Krak des Chevaliers, a castle that
had been held for Christendom for
161 years, fell to the Saracens.

Krak des Chevaliers in Syria was captured
by the Hospitallers in the 11th century, and
rebuilt into one of the most sophisticated
Crusader castles of its time.

Castles of America

The Americas could hardly be considered a land of castles or strongholds with perhaps the exception of the occasional military fort in former Spanish-held regions, and some relics of past conquests in Latin America. Yet the United States has its own castles, its own reasons for building them, and its own reasons for venerating them.

Compared with the historic piles of Europe, mellowed through centuries of existence, most of the castles in America are of course, new, lacking in the expected savage background; unblooded, unbesieged, unslighted. Few have seen the clash of arms. They are, cynics might declare, merely the pretentious homes of the pretentious rich.

It does not matter that the cynics are in essence, correct. These homes, some built to resemble castles by owners whose flights of imagination were fulfilled through such building, others raised faithfully to the style, if not the detail, of a castle extant, are the products of a small coterie of people with the common goal of creating their own history, and bound together in a protest against the architectural geometry of their time. The majority were built at the turn of the 19th century, an age of rapid and ruthless industrial expansion in America, and were the concrete manifestations of a yearning for another age. And if the cynic cares to thumb his nose at these dwellings as mere crenellated mock-antique or English collegiate Gothic one may answer – give them time. They will assimilate history, or have it thrust upon them, or make their own, and will probably still be there mellowing like their European forebears.

Castillo De San Marcos

Is a castle that can claim some 300 years of active history, in Saint Augustine, Florida, which was then a Spanish possession. A pirate raid in 1668 encouraged the inhabitants to build a stone fortress. The Spanish Queen Regent, Marianna, directed that the Viceroy of Mexico provide the funds for a permanent stronghold, similar to those protecting Spanish territories in the Caribbean for all the earlier ones along the Florida coast had been made of wood, and had soon deteriorated in the moist sea air. The work of construction began in the autumn of 1672, the labour being mainly slaves and Indian workmen who ferried huge coquina blocks by barge to the fort's seaboard site.

San Marcos slowly progressed despite further raids by English pirates and after twenty-four years of toil under the hot Florida sun, the fortress was finished, a grim and impregnable citadel that still holds

The northernmost outpost of Spain's former Caribbean empire, Castillo San Marcos, Florida, is a forceful reminder of the 235 years of Spanish presence in the United States.

visitors in awe as they contemplate the cost in labour and the countless lost lives of peon workmen.

Biltmore House

At first glance this could be a château de plaisance of 16th century France. With its late Gothic façade, its tall slate roofs, spiral staircase and ornate chimneys it has the air of a miniature Chambord or Fontainebleau, with here and there a feature from Chenonceau or Blois. And in fact this was the effect that its builder George Washington Vanderbilt wished to produce.

Vanderbilt had noticed, on one of his rides through the countryside of western North Carolina, a spot which had one of the finest views in the region. He decided to buy the land – some 125,000 acres of it – and build a château there in the fashion of Francis I, the French monarch whose 16th century architectural works may still be seen today on the banks of the Loire.

Two of the most distinguished

architects in America were called in to plan the estate and George Vanderbilt, himself a student of architecture, chose the historic style. Richard Hunt, who was to design the building itself, had already produced palatial residences for a number of America's wealthy families, and had earlier completed a château-style mansion on Fifth Avenue for William K. Vanderbilt that had proved a milestone for both family and architect.

Like several of the Loire châteaux, Biltmore, completed in 1895, lies in gentle rolling country with its river winding through its lower grounds. The dimensions of the château itself are comparable to those of a large French château, with a front elevation of some 238 metres (780 feet) in length. Its Gothic elements – windows, doors, pinnacles, gargoyles and chimneys are ordered by a basic plan of Renaissance symmetry. The famed architect and artist Frederick Olnsted landscaped the vast grounds.

Inside, décor and style has been drawn from several centuries. Rooms in the mode of Louis XV and Louis XVI, furniture of the Jacobean period, of the time of Francis I and later, are of particular interest to the historian. The tall

arched banqueting hall is over 21 metres (70 feet) long and hung with fine 16th century tapestries. Bedrooms are sympathetically decorated in several historic styles, and the library is one of the most impressive in the State.

Today Biltmore, owned by George and William Vanderbilt, grandsons of its builder, run the estate commercially, although part of its original land, deeded some time ago to the Department of the Interior, is now the Pisgah National Forest. Agricultural projects such as forestry, arable and dairy farming (about 2,000 cows graze the land) help to make the estate self-sufficient now, and since 1930 the grounds and house have been open to the public as a National Historic Landmark.

George W. Vanderbilt wanted to build America's finest home. He also succeeded in creating America's finest château, symbol of gracious living on the grand scale.

The library at Biltmore House is furnished in Baroque style and contains over 20,000 volumes on its shelves.

Abbadia Mare

Some 200 years younger, but looking very medieval indeed, is Hammond Castle, at Gloucester, Massachusetts, a solid edifice complete with towers and turrets, battlements and drawbridge, designed and built by one of America's most prolific inventors, John Hays Hammond (1888–1965), a man whose patents are still very much part of the American remote-control radio scene. One of his early experiments is still remembered with awe at Gloucester Bay when local fishermen watched in speechless astonishment as a crewless boat was manoeuvred around the bay, controlled from the shore by radio.

One of this century's most brilliant inventors yet relatively unknown, Hammond was also

Above: The high arched banqueting hall in Biltmore House.

Left: The eastern elevation of Biltmore house in Ashville, North Carolina. Built for George Washington Vanderbilt between 1889 and 1895, this magnificent château is an amalgam of many features to be seen in 16th century châteaux in France.

keenly interested in the art world, and resolved to construct a home in which he could display some of his accumulated treasures. In 1925 he started work on a large stone castle that was to be an elaborate art-and-science centre.

Apart from offices and laboratories – functional units constructed in modern idiom – the majority of the building was in 12th century style, with fortified towers of the period, a great hall that was designed in 14th century manner and domestic quarters in the form of the 15th century.

Called Abbadia Mare, Abbey by the Sea, Hammond's Gothic castle had a more feudal than ecclesiastic appearance, with its heavy chain-supported pont-levis flanked by fierce leonine figures, and with a barred inspection hatch in the massive entrance door. Treasures

Hammond Castle, Abbadia Mare, at Gloucester, Massachusetts, once the home of one of America's most brilliant electronic scientists.

The Great Hall at Hammond Castle, built in 1925 but looking exactly like a product of the Middle Ages.

from medieval Germany, furniture from the France of Louis IV, a 12th century Christ in wood, an entire house-façade from 14th century Amiens, an organ with ten thousand pipes, a priceless Madonna, a 5th century sarcophagus from Rome . . . Abbadia Mare is a castle crammed with the treasures of the world, a unique collection that is open today to all who wish to see them.

Scotty's Castle

Near the border of California and Nevada, Death Valley, now a National Park, is mostly desert with small scrub punctuating the brown hills. Tucked down between the Last Chance Range and the Bullfrog Hills at Death Valley's northern end, Scotty's Castle spreads out like a Spanish urbanization – a cluster of low red-topped buildings designed to fend off the blazing sun and capture as much life-giving shade as

possible. Once a flourishing mining area, Death Valley is now a still, silent, arid region so empty that there are more traces of the Ice Age to be seen there than of human habitation.

The red-tiled 'castle', with its numerous rooms in styles that include some bizarre Spanish Classic mixed with Scottish Gothic was begun in 1922. Intended as a holiday retreat for wealthy mid-westerner Albert Johnson, the castle was built at the suggestion of his close friend Walter Scott, who knew the area well. When Johnson died, 'Scotty' lived at the castle for the six remaining years of his life, until 1958.

Since 1970 Scotty's Castle (which was known as Death Valley Ranch to its original owners) has been the property of the U.S. Government, part of the fascinating 3,000 square mile Death Valley National Monument.

More a ranch than a fortress, 'Scotty's Castle' in Death Valley on the border of California and Nevada, is situated in one of the hottest and driest parts of the U.S.A.

Hearst Castle

San Simeon, California, is still a name that conjures up fascinating memories. William Randolph Hearst, the megalomaniac empire-building newspaper tycoon was a compulsive collector of anything he thought valuable, bizarre or unique in the art world. And he was the owner of some quarter of a million acres of land near San Simeon Bay, a ranch called Piedra Blanca.

On this enormous spread was an elevated plateau, a place of special meaning for young Hearst who had spent much of his vigorous youth there when his family had used it as a camp site. It was an 'enchanted hill', he later wrote. Here he built his luxurious rambling home, Hearst Castle. In addition to living in it, he used it to house the mountains of art objects he had accumulated during his years of voracious collecting.

copper, and dazzling white towers flanked the façade. Inside, 17th century Flemish tapestries draped the fireplaces in the great assembly hall, whose heavy coffered ceiling had been transported from Italy and installed intact. Gilded doors allowed guests to proceed to the refectory, cool under its 400-year-old ceiling of dark wood brought directly from a medieval monastery. At one end of the room a tall mantelpiece from a French château looks haughtily down on diners while at the other end, a musicians' gallery awaits its musicians. A small elevator leading to Hearst's private quarters is concealed behind a wall panel. A small study in Gothic décor, perhaps the most beautiful room in the castle, is supported by Spanish Gothic arches and embellished with painted medieval scenes.

During the building of the castle Hearst's constant companion was

As a young boy his mother had taken him to Europe, where he had been fascinated by the ancient and historic castles of France and Germany, and had developed a passion for beautiful and expensive things. In 1919 Hearst began work on the first of three guest-houses at San Simeon, then started on the main building, La Casa Grande, changing his mind and his plans frequently as work progressed.

Campaniles pointed their fingers to the sky, filigreed windows in marble abounded, pilasters and balustrades supported domes of

the Brooklyn-born showgirl Marion Davies. Hearst was over fifty and she just twenty-one. She was with him on many of his art-collecting tours in Europe and must have been an influence in much that he brought back to his amazing museum of antique and unique objects.

The world of letters, of politics, of art came to stay in Hearst's magic castle. Men of the calibre of Churchill and Shaw; people from the stage – Flynn, Chaplin, Keaton, Lombard were fascinated by this man of talent and immense wealth.

But time moved on. Vast tracts of the land were used during the last war as a training ground for troops. In 1946 an ailing Hearst moved to a more modest abode on the advice of his physician. In 1951 he died. He left his castle and its fabled contents to the State of California. It was opened to the public in 1958.

Above: Newspaper magnate William Hearst built this vast castle-residence on a hill near San Simeon Bay, California.

Far left: The dining hall or refectory at San Simeon, cool under its 400-year-old ceiling.

Bottom left: The Spanish-classic entrance portico of Hearst's San Simeon.

Right: Old San Juan, an islet off the shore of mainland Puerto Rico, was founded in 1521. The castle of El Morro, seen here in the foreground of the picture, commands the harbour entrance, the oldest defence structure on this historic island. Old San Juan has three castles defending its minute area – San Cristobel, El Canuelo and El Morro.

Glossary

Archière An arrow slit in a castle wall.

Bailey The area enclosed within a curtain wall or palisade. In it would be outbuildings such as kitchens and stables.

Barbican Masonry outwork built to protect the approach to a castle.

Barmkin The outer fortification of a castle.

Bartizan Small overhanging turret on a wall or tower.

Bastide Anglaise A town fortified during the 12th century by the English as an outpost.

Bastion Fortified projection occurring at intervals in a castle wall.

Battlements An indented parapet with a series of openings used to protect archers.

Berquil Large outdoor reservoir found in Crusader and Arab castles.

Castellan The official commanding officer and governor of a castle.

Castellation Battlements used as a decorative feature.

Chemise A wall around a keep.

Concentric castle A central fortress ringed by a series of outer curtain walls.

Corbel A stone or brick projection from a wall to provide a horizontal support.

Cour d'honneur Reception courtyard of a château.

Crenellation See **Castellation.**

Curtain wall Main outer defence wall of a castle's fortifications. It is not itself the wall of a building though it may be protected by towers and turrets.

Donjon See **Keep.**

Embrasures The openings between the merlons, forming crenellations.

Enceinte The entire circuit of a curtain wall.

Garderobe Latrine or privy.

Keep The main tower or stronghold of a castle.

Machicolation A stone projection on top of a castle wall with floor holes through which missiles were dropped.

Merlon The rising masonry wall on a battlement.

Motte A natural or artificial mound within the castle walls.

Motte-and-bailey castle Name given to a type of castle widespread in Britain and Normandy during the 10th and 11th centuries. In its simplest form it consisted of a motte surrounded by a palisade enclosing the bailey.

Meutrière Loophole in a fortification for the discharge of missiles against the enemy outside.

Oubliette A secret dungeon with an opening only at the top.

Palisade A fence of stakes surrounding a castle or defensive position.

Pont-levis Drawbridge of a castle.

Portcullis Iron-clad wooden grill made to slide vertically in grooved channels in the gateway of a castle to prevent entrance and provide additional protection.

Ward An area of a castle's defences.

Yett Scottish for 'gate'.